WE BELIEVE AND TEACH

Martin J. Heinecken

Edited by Harold W. Rast

Fortress Press, Philadelphia

Lead Books

Lead Books are prepared under the direction of the Division for Parish Services, the Lutheran Church in America.

Unless otherwise noted, Scripture quotations in this publication are from the *Revised Standard Version Common Bible*, copyrighted © 1973. The quotation of Ephesians 1:9–12 in Chapter Two is from *The New Testament in Modern English*, copyright J. B. Phillips 1958, 1960, 1972. Used by permission of The Macmillan Company, publisher in the U.S.A., and Geoffrey Bles Ltd., London, publisher for all other parts of the English-speaking world.

Quotations from Luther's *Small Catechism* are from the 1979 edition of *The Small Catechism by Martin Luther, in Contemporary English with Lutheran Book of Worship Texts* and have been used by permission. Quotations from *The Book of Concord* are from the 1959 edition translated by Theodore G. Tappert and copyrighted by Fortress Press, Philadelphia, Pennsylvania.

Art and design by Terry O'Brien.

Second printing 1983

Library of Congress Cataloging in Publication Data

Heinecken, Martin J.
  We believe and teach.

  (Lead books)
  1. Theology, Doctrinal. I. Rast, Harold W.
II. Title. III. Series.
BT75.2.H44   230   80-16363
ISBN 0-8006-1387-2

K395A83   Printed in U.S.A.   1-1387

CONTENTS

FOREWORD

"Believing does not mean you should stop thinking," says a heading in *The Faith Letters* by Helmut Thielicke. "Faith is something it pays to think about," Thielicke adds, "and the person who believes keeps on thinking."

We Believe and Teach has been written for persons who believe and who are willing to keep on thinking about what they believe.

Knowing, understanding, and thinking about the teachings of Christianity, however, are not ends in themselves. They are, instead, the means to an end—the means which lead to stronger belief, faith, and trust in the redeeming work of Jesus the Christ.

We Believe and Teach is not a simple how-to book. It takes effort to read and understand. But that effort will ultimately prove worthwhile. The lofty, awesome, inspiring, and joyful world of thinking about God has its own rewards, as readers will discover.

Alpha and Omega—
The Beginning and the End

"I am the first and I am the last; besides me there is no god."

Isaiah 44:6

Chapter One
GOD MAKES HIMSELF KNOWN

Who is God and what is God like? How does a person come to know God? What can we learn about God from the things he has made? How do people confuse God with what he has made? What does the Bible tell us about God? How valuable is the Bible's witness? What is the meaning of the term *Word of God*? How does God continue to make himself known today?

The word *god*

A college professor once said to a freshman student, "Some people will tell you there is a god, others that there is not. I'd like to assure you, however, that the truth lies somewhere in between."

We laugh at this story because we believe there can be no "in between." Either there is a god or there is not. Suggesting something "in between" is just a clever way of avoiding the question.

Actually, all of our questions about God make no sense until we explain what we mean by the word. Most people, even those who deny there is a god, have a definite conception of God. Perhaps they have in mind a vengeful tribal god who arbitrarily plays favorites and whose anger must be appeased with human sacrifices. If so, that's the kind of god whose existence they will deny. Or they may have the notion of a supreme being who accounts for order and beauty in the universe. In this case they will likely affirm the existence of this kind of god. Examples like these could be multiplied many times over.

Since people load the term *God* with many different meanings, we will have to determine what these meanings have in common. Our question is simply, What do people really mean when they use the word god?

Your god

Martin Luther claimed that everyone worships either the true God or an idol. He said in his *Large Catechism* that where a person's heart is, there is that person's god. "That to which your heart clings and entrusts itself is . . . really your God." Luther meant that everyone actually has a god because everyone worships or ascribes worth to someone or something. Persons may worship their spouses, children, fame, money, sex, power, success, or anything that becomes a ruling concern for them. In all of these cases, however, they may really be worshiping only themselves.

That to which people ascribe supreme worth and that which *actually* rules their lives, no matter what else they may profess, is their god. The word god may therefore be defined as that which people make the object of their worship and to which they give their highest allegiance.

If it is true that there is only one God who alone is worthy of worship and supreme allegiance, then as Luther said, everyone worships either that one true God or an idol. If people do not worship the one true God, they worship a false god who is not worthy of their worship or allegiance. God told the people of Israel, "I am the Lord your God, who brought you out of the land of Egypt, out of the house of bondage. You shall have no other gods before me" (Exodus 20: 2–3). Luther said this passage means that "we are to fear, love, and trust God above anything else."

And Jesus said "You shall love the Lord your God with all your heart, and with all your soul, and with all your mind" (Matthew 22:37; see also 4:10).

God's disclosure

The words for God in the Exodus and Matthew passages are the same in both instances. Each of these passages presupposes that God has already made himself known as a particular kind of being. He has revealed who he is and that he cares about humankind. God has shown himself to be worthy of worship.

God is the "Lord God" according to Exodus and Matthew. In Hebrew, the language of the Old Testament, the word for Lord is *Yahweh* (YAH-way) and the word for God is *Elohim* (el-low-HEEM). Both of these words or names have a specific meaning.

When Moses heard the voice from the flaming bush telling him to lead his people out of Egypt, he asked who he should say had sent him. "What is his name?" The voice answered: "I am who I am (Yahweh). Say this to the people of Israel, 'I am (Yahweh) has sent me to you'" (Exodus 3:13–14). This suggests that God is consistent with his nature, not capricious, and faithful to his word. A better, more complete translation of Yahweh is: *I am not a God who is far away, unable to hear the cries of my people or unwilling to answer their cries; I am a God who is near, who hears their cries, and who is both willing and able to help.*

The other name we need to discuss is Elohim, which means "the power of powers." When placed next to Yahweh, as in the phrase "the Lord (Yahweh) your God (Elohim)," this name suggests that Yahweh really has the power to carry out the promised deliverance of his people and never to let them down. The "Lord God" is the "deliverer God" who is concerned about his people; he has the power out of sheer grace to rescue them. Therefore he alone is to be worshiped and to receive supreme allegiance. Moreover, it is this same "Lord God" who is revealed in a unique, once-for-all, complete way in Jesus the Christ, our Deliverer from the bondage of sin.

God's face

God never shows his face. The Bible says that the "Lord God" deliberately never shows his face. God never appears to finite, limited, sinful people in his naked glory. If he did, they would die. God said to Moses, "You cannot see my face; for man shall not see me and live" (Exodus 33:20). In the New Testament we read, "No one has ever seen God; the only Son, who is the bosom of the Father, he has made him known" (John 1:18; see also 1 John 4:20).

According to the Bible, then, to be a creature of God means to fear, love, trust, and obey an *unseen God.* That's what Adam and Eve, as representatives of the human race, were asked to do. Their challenge was to take God at his word, to heed his warning, and to believe his promises. Because they did not do this, they lost their paradise. Likewise, as we will see, the entire human race lost its paradise because it too failed to trust the unseen God.

As humans we are not able to see God in his glory face to face. We have no idea what God in his glory looks like. Such a vision is reserved for the day when time as we now know it is over.

In the meantime God remains the hidden God. Any notion of a directly visible god, who can be universally recognized as God because he is so different and unusual, is a heathen notion. Such a god is actually an idol. God does not appear in some unusual, striking form like the pagan gods, but remains hidden within the created world.

The masks of creation

God is not distant or aloof from his creation, but is present everywhere in it. Psalm 139 reminds us that there is nowhere we can flee from his presence. Nevertheless,

God's presence is and remains hidden. Luther therefore spoke of masks that God uses to cover and clothe himself so that we may be able to bear and comprehend him. God is the One to whom we owe everything we have and are (1 Corinthians 4:7). He has created us and provides us with all that we need for life. But he does not do any of this directly. He gives us light and energy through the sun. He gives us life through our parents. He gives us food from the earth, which has been made fruitful by the rain (Psalm 104). He delights us through the beauty of the sunset and through the work of musicians and artists of all kinds; he makes us laugh through the clown in the circus. So the whole creation—everything in it, including all we can see, touch, feel, smell—is like a stage full of masked creatures in whom the unseen and unseeable God is present.

These masks are not themselves God; they effectively hide the God who is "in, with, and under" the earthly elements. If we do not make a clear distinction between the Creator and the creature, we might be considered pantheists, that is, persons who claim that the universe itself is God. However, because of this clear distinction, we can greet the sun as it rises in all its splendor with "Good morning, Lord!" instead of with the pessimist's growl, "Good Lord, morning!"

The Scottish theologian, John Baillie, coined the phrase "mediated immediacy" to describe the hidden presence of God. God is present, closer than hands and feet, but always in a medium that effectively hides his glory so we may be able to bear it.

We have said that the masks of creation effectively hide God's presence. As every masquerader knows, however, though a mask effectively hides, it also reveals in a most tantalizing way. Think of eyes peering through and the shape of the mask, possibly indicating the contour of a face. These help you make guesses about the identity of the hidden one. By the same token, the actions of the masquerader will most certainly tell you something about him or her (for example, whether he or she is a good dancer or a clod). But the true identity of the masquerader is not revealed until the ball is over and the mask has been removed. Then is the time for surprises. So will it be on the last day when God finally removes his mask and we see him face to face.

Experiencing "the holy"

Have you ever felt you were in the uncanny presence of something that both frightened and attracted you? What about the vast night sky and its numberless stars? Or the mountains with their dizzying heights? Or the restless waves of the ocean with the vast horizon all around? Or the fury of a storm, the howling wind, the thunder and lightning (even though you know what is causing these . . . or do you). Or the roaring, tumbling waters of Niagara? Or, to change the scenario, the song of a hermit thrush, a symphony in miniature? Or a field of wild flowers, a rainbow, a baby's smile, a beautiful male or female person, a human hand?

The list could go on and on and, with each item, the awareness or sense of the unknown. Is it good or evil? Is nothing there other than what the eye can see, the ear hear, the nose smell, the hand feel?

The hidden presence of God in his creation leads to the universal experience of what has been called "the holy." *Holy* suggests words like "whole" and "healthy"; it has come to mean for us primarily being free from fault and possessing all the so-called virtues. We think of a holy God who never does wrong, a God who is always clean and spotless, a God who is perfect in every way. As a television character used to say, "God din't make no mistakes. That's how he come to be God."

God is holy; he is free from and in opposition to all that is evil in the world. God's holiness, therefore, can be associated with his wrath. The holy God cannot tolerate anyone or anything that is evil.

13

The word holy also suggests something wholly other or different from anything you have ever seen—something completely unknown and shrouded in mystery. To know that something is there, but to have no idea what it is, creates fear and trembling. It also attracts and fascinates. Hence "the holy" has been called "the mystery that both attracts and repels." This is what the unknown always does.

Suppose you receive a package that gives no identification or clue concerning its contents. It's a truly mysterious package. Wouldn't you be fascinated and irresistibly drawn to open it? Wouldn't you also be apprehensive and reluctant to open it because it might contain a bomb or a priceless treasure?

People have felt this way about unexplored places they believed were inhabited by mysterious forces. Eventually these places came to be regarded as holy places, where people could bring offerings to appease, give thanks, or win the favor of unknown powers.

A similar attitude prevailed about the mysterious forces of nature—the sun, the sea, the storm, the mountains, the sky. People assumed that there were other unknown powers behind what was accessible to the senses. They therefore attributed the quality of holiness to all these powers at whose mercy they felt themselves, and they expressed both grateful thanksgiving and groveling fear toward them. All of this may be understood as encounter with the hidden God in the masks of creation.

Finally, the experience of "the holy" is universal. It is the experience not just of superstitious people, but of all people of all times. It is the experience also of those who have reached the highest possible levels of learning, of people who live in the space age and who have penetrated formerly dark and unknown places.

The sense of "the holy" accompanies the experience of God when he does reveal himself. When God draws aside the veil, we know more is there than meets the eye. The mystery of God is not solved, to be sure, but only heightened. This was true of Isaiah's vision in the Temple of the Holy One of Israel. The prophet saw the Lord high and lifted up and heard the angel hosts singing, "Holy, holy, holy is the LORD of hosts; the whole earth is full of his glory" (Isaiah 6:3). The account of the prophet's vision continues: "And the foundations of the thresholds shook at the voice of him who called, and the house was filled with smoke. And I [Isaiah] said: 'Woe is me! For I am lost; for I am a man of unclean lips, and I dwell in the midst of a people of unclean lips; for my eyes have seen the King, the LORD of hosts!' " (Isaiah 6:4–5). Yet with all this dramatic experience of "the holy" and this vision of the Lord of hosts, we are given no description of God.

Think also of what happened to people, even the disciples, when Jesus performed miracles. While the miracles were not intended to prove that Jesus is God, they nevertheless created a sense of "the holy" among those who witnessed them. For example, after Jesus stilled the storm the disciples "were filled with awe, and said to one another, 'Who then is this, that even the wind and sea obey him?' " (Mark 4:41; see also Matthew 27:54; 28:5; Luke 1:13–31; 2:10).

God confronts us

God is present but hidden in the masks of creation. His nature is disclosed there to a certain extent, but never in its fulness. God's disclosure in the masks of creation always remains somewhat ambiguous.

The untold blessings which creation provides, however, say something about God. Consider the order, beauty, and surpassing wonder of the world. With our reason, we conclude that a wise and beneficent architect must be involved. We think it unlikely that all this happened by chance. A well-ordered house containing so many good things for a happy life implies a clever builder and a gracious host—even if he never shows his face!

15

In addition, humankind discovers that laws exist for the control of society and the orderly operation of the physical universe. Observing these laws rather than violating them, we conclude, makes for human well-being.

People also experience a sense of obligation within themselves, which leads them to regard certain kinds of behavior as good and other kinds as evil. This suggests to the human mind that someone or something must be responsible for the existence of moral order in the universe.

Yet all of the disorder, ugliness, pain, suffering, injustice, and evil in the world make people skeptical. Could it be that a blundering idiot or an evil genius made the world and is now playing madly with the controls? The exact opposite of a just moral order often seems true, that is, that might makes right and injustice triumphs.

In short, by thinking and examining the available evidence in creation, humankind cannot on its own discover the true nature of that mysterious power or being upon which it feels dependent. Nor can humankind certify God's existence.

It is one thing for people to sit, think, and draw conclusions about an "architect of the universe," "a supreme being," or someone responsible for moral order in the universe. These ideas may be interesting and logical, but they are merely products of people's thinking about God. They are not God. Ideas cannot address persons, hold them responsible, and call them to give thanks.

The situation is quite different if it is God himself who confronts us in the masks of creation and calls upon us to give thanks. Then we are personally involved with the living God himself, not just with our thoughts or ideas about God.

Typical human response

According to biblical history (for example, Isaiah 40:12–31; 44:9–11; also Acts 14:1–18 and Romans

1:18–32), the typical human response to God's hidden presence in creation is to confuse the Creator and creature, and to worship the creature rather than the Creator. In the course of history, people have worshiped the actual forces of nature. They have made gods of the sun, sea, and rain. Think of the pantheon of Greek gods who supposedly lived on Mt. Olympus: Jupiter, the chief of the gods; Hermes, the messenger of the gods; Zephyrus, god of the west wind. The ancients surrounded these gods with the aura of holiness. They also made images of the powers upon which they felt dependent and worshiped them.

The Bible holds people responsible for the confusion of Creator and creature. According to Acts 14, the people took Paul and Barnabas to be gods after they had healed a crippled man. The people, in fact, wanted to offer sacrifices to these early missionaries. But Paul and Barnabas protested this false worship, claiming to be mere human beings like all the rest. They tried to turn the people from worshiping the creature to worshiping the living God who made all creatures. Though God is not visible, they told the people, he "did not leave himself without witness, for he did good and gave you from heaven rains and fruitful seasons, satisfying your hearts with food and gladness" (Acts 14:17). Through his hidden presence in creation, God had confronted the people and called upon them to worship him, to acknowledge him as God, and to give thanks.

In Romans 1, Paul says that all people are under God's judgment and wrath and are without excuse. Why? Because "what can be known about God is plain to them, because God has shown it to them. Ever since the creation of the world his invisible nature, namely, his eternal power and deity, has been clearly perceived in the things that have been made. So they are without excuse; for although they knew God they did not honor him as God or give thanks to him" (Romans 1:19–21). They worshiped the creature rather than the Creator. God therefore let them suffer the consequences of turning the created order upside down.

What this means, then, is that the loving God, the Holy One, the Creator who is never to be confused with the creature, confronts all people and calls upon them to acknowledge him as God who alone is worthy of their worship. Unfortunately, people fail to do this; instead, they worship the creature and not the Creator. This may involve them in crude idolatry, bowing down either to images made by their own hands or to personifications of the forces of nature. They may also worship the creature rather than the Creator by giving their hearts to persons or things in the created world.

This is true also of you and me. Besides being confronted by God in the teachings of our Christian parents and the church or in reading the Bible and other Christian testimony, we are also constantly confronted by God in the masks of creation. We are called again and again to acknowledge and worship him alone, to thank and serve him. Yet like all the people of the world, we turn to and worship the creature rather than the Creator. For example, our material possessions may be more important to us than God from whom comes "every good endowment and every perfect gift" (James 1:17). We are therefore without excuse, and the wrath of God rightly rests also upon us. Furthermore, God allows us to suffer the consequences of turning his created order upside down.

Bible events

The many blessings of life and the creation can lead us to conclude that God is wise, powerful, and good. At the same time, however, we recognize that there are many evils and injustices in the world. The witness in creation, therefore, cannot by itself lead us to the conclusion that God is an inexhaustible fountain of sheer love, which he freely pours out upon the undeserving, even the enemy.

To reveal himself to humankind as the God of unconditional love and to save people from their idolatry, God acted in that series of events to which the Bible witnesses. The Bible is, in fact, the book of the acts of God who revealed himself finally and supremely in Jesus the Christ. All other conceptions of God must be judged, corrected, and fulfilled by God's revelation in Jesus.

God, then, is the revealed God. People do not discover him through their own ingenuity or clever brains. God takes the initiative and deliberately draws aside the veil to show us what he is like. However, even this is done through a "mediated immediacy," so that God in his naked glory never appears, not even in the person of Jesus.

The people of Israel

"How odd of God to choose the Jews" wrote William Norman Ewer in the early 1900s. We cannot possibly know why God chose a particular people among whom to reveal himself in a special way, at special times, and in special places. The fact is that all human history and all creation is the arena for God's self-disclosure. However, God chose to act particularly within the life and history of the Israelite people, to set in motion a series of events that would reach fulfillment in the new age of Jesus the Christ.

The choice of the particular people of Israel has to be seen by looking back to Jesus of Nazareth as the center of all history. And Jesus cannot properly be understood except against the background of the Old Testament and the choice of Israel. The New Testament will always be misunderstood unless seen as the fulfillment of the Old. The record of God's saving acts in history narrows down to Jesus the center, then spreads out from that center to the ends of the earth and to the end of the age. Jesus' genealogy in Matthew 1:1–16 goes back to Abraham; in Luke 3:23–38 it is carried all the way back to Adam as the representative of the human race. The coming of the wise men (Matthew 2:1–12) indicates that there were signs everywhere pointing to the birth of the One to whom every knee should bow.

Prophets and apostles

The Bible records the acts of God, specifically the choice and liberation of the people of Israel and his dealings with them until finally, in the fulness of time, God sent his Son to "save his people from their sins" (Matthew 1:21). In other words, God's revelation is historical. He makes known his will and ways through mighty and gracious acts in history.

But God and his purposes for humankind would remain essentially hidden had he *only* acted. Therefore, God has provided interpretations of his acts through the prophets of the Old Testament and the apostles of the New. Amos 3:7 says, "Surely the Lord God does nothing, without revealing his secret to his servants the prophets." God makes himself known through actions plus God-given interpretations.

The Bible

The Bible is the record of God's acts and their interpretation. Therefore, the Bible has been called the Word of God and has been regarded as inspired by him and able to inspire us (2 Timothy 3:14–17; 2 Peter 1:19–21). However, scarcely anything in our day has caused more confusion and division than calling the Bible the Word of God. At one extreme are those who think that God inspired every word of the Bible, as though dictating to a secretary. Consequently, they argue, every sentence and word in the Bible is absolutely true because it is God's Word. At the other extreme are those who regard the Bible as no different from any other book that provides inspiration for living. They may place it at the top of the list, but it is still only one inspirational book among many. In between are all kinds of other opinions, with most people still tending to think that if it is in the Bible, it must be true. The word *Bible* has, in fact, come to mean the authoritative and final word, as for example, "The Bible of Golfers."

The nature and function of the Bible is an important and complicated issue that requires separate study. Here we will only briefly summarize our understanding of the Bible as Word of God.

Jesus the Word of God

The Word of God is, in its most important sense, the Word become flesh in Jesus the Christ. "Word of God," then, is an expression that can be reserved almost exclusively for Jesus. It is an expression that should make us think of Jesus rather than of the Bible. We sing in a well-known hymn, "O Word of God Incarnate." Moreover, the writer of Hebrews says: "In many and various ways God spoke of old to our fathers by the prophets; but in these last days he has spoken to us by a Son . . . He [the Son] reflects the glory of God and bears the very stamp of his nature, upholding the universe by his word of power" (Hebrews 1:1–3). John 1:1 and 14 is even more explicit: "In the beginning was the Word, and the Word was with God, and the Word was God. . . . And the Word became flesh and dwelt among us, full of grace and truth; we have beheld his glory, glory as of the only Son from the Father."

God's living voice

Since Jesus Christ is God's Word, that is, God's gracious personal message to humankind, we may apply the term Word of God to anything in which this message is found. The Word of God is, in fact, the living voice of the gospel proclaimed with sufficiency and power no matter where (in church or elsewhere) or by whom (ordained clergy or lay people). The Word of God spreads as living witnesses carry it to the ends of the earth and to the end of the age. All that is necessary for spreading the Word are living witnesses who faithfully proclaim it to hearers throughout the world.

Written record and oral witness

The Bible is testimony literature. It witnesses to what God has said and done.

The first witness was oral. The prophets spoke directly to the people; only later were their messages written down. Jesus himself wrote nothing. For years after his death and resurrection there was no written record, no stenographic account, no videotape. The witness was simply passed by word of mouth.

The necessity of a written record became apparent (see Luke 1:1–4). In the course of time both the Old and New Testaments came into being and took the form in which we now have them. It is not possible, therefore, to suppose that there was one original version which was word-for-word inspired of God and absolutely inerrant. The earliest manuscripts we have of the Bible, for example, contain thousands and thousands of variations in the wording of Scripture passages. All scholars can hope to do is establish a text that may have a degree of accuracy. Establishing texts is a matter of probability, not of absolute certainty. Yet these written witnesses are the only record we have regarding what happened and what was said in the past. So we must rely on them.

The written record is vital for the continuation of the oral witness. All churches that acknowledge Jesus as the Christ agree on that. The Roman Catholic Church, for example, regards the decisions of the "teaching magisterium" (the bishops with the pope as head) as authoritative interpretations of the Scriptures, not as completely independent decisions.

Protestant churches throughout the world accept the Holy Scriptures as authoritative in matters of faith and life.

For example, the Constitution of Lutheran Church in America states: "This church acknowledges the Holy Scriptures as the norm for the faith and life of the Church. The Holy Scriptures are the divinely inspired record of God's redemptive act in Christ, for which the Old Testament prepared the way and which the New Testament proclaims. In the continuation of this proclamation in the church, God still speaks through the Holy Scriptures and realizes His redemptive purpose generation after generation."

The Bible contains . . .

Some people like to say that the Bible only contains the Word of God. They imply that only certain parts of it are the Word while the rest are just human words. This is like having a bushel of apples that you divide into good and bad piles by sniffing, touching, and tasting them. In a somewhat similar manner, persons could set themselves up as judges and pick out of the Bible what suits their own tastes. For example, they might readily accept as God's Word the psalmist's longing for Jerusalem: "By the waters of Babylon, there we sat down and wept, when we remembered Zion. . . . How shall we sing the Lord's song in a foreign land? . . . Let my tongue cleave to the roof of my mouth . . . if I do not set Jerusalem above my highest joy!" (Psalm 137:1–6). On the other hand, they might vehemently reject those terribly vengeful words against the Edomites which conclude this psalm: "Happy shall he be who takes your little ones and dashes them against the rock!" (Psalm 137:9).

But who are we to make these judgments, lapping up words of comfort and rejecting words that cry to high heaven against treacherous deeds that somehow should be avenged? The Edomites, after all, had betrayed their blood brothers, the Israelites. Instead of coming to the Israelites' aid against invading hordes, the Edomites stood by and cheered the fall of Jerusalem. Then, when the battle was over, they turned into ghouls to rob the bodies of the dead—a particularly repulsive deed in any case. And how shall the cross of Christ, in which the infinite sufferings of God himself atone for the sins of the world, have any unique and incomparable significance if it is not true, "Vengeance is mine, I will repay, says the Lord" (Romans 12:19)? It is therefore not legitimate for us to set ourselves up as judges over Scripture. Instead, we should try to hear what it has to say to us when read in the proper context, to hear even such offensive things as maledictions against the Edomites or seemingly inconsequential matters like genealogies.

The Bible does not become the Word

To say that the Bible becomes the Word of God, like a dead wire which becomes live only when the current is turned on, can also lead to misunderstanding. Nevertheless, the Bible may be said to be the Word of God in somewhat the same way. A Bible lying covered with dust in the old family parlor, of course, is not going to perform any dynamics. Or a New Testament worn over the heart will not necessarily protect one from machine gun bullets. Still, Jesus was the Word become flesh even when he slept, washed, dressed, and ate. He did not only become the Word of God when he spoke and someone proved responsive to his word. It is the same with the Bible. In one sense the Bible is always the Word of God, whether we use it and respond to it or not. This, however, should not lead us to make the Bible a kind of sacred object that we worship.

The expression "The Bible becomes the Word of God" intends to make a valid point, that is, that reading the printed page or hearing the proclaimed Word does not necessarily accomplish anything. A word must always be understood according to its intended meaning if it is to accomplish its purpose. This is true in a particular sense of the words of the Bible. They speak to you as the Word of

God only as the Holy Spirit works in and through them. The writer of Ephesians, therefore, encourages us to take "the sword of the Spirit, which is the word of God" (Ephesians 6:17). And Hebrews explains: "For the word of God is living and active, sharper than any two-edged sword, piercing to the division of soul and spirit, of joints and marrow, and discerning the thoughts and intentions of the heart. And before him no creature is hidden, but all are open and laid bare to the eyes of him with whom we have to do" (Hebrews 4:12–13). It is not up to us to say which words or parts of the Bible will manifest this power in the Holy Spirit, or when or how.

Divine and human word

We may, indeed, say that the Bible is the Word of God, but only paradoxically so since it is, at the same time, always the word of human beings. Paradoxically means "counter to appearance" as well as "counter to the general opinion." The Bible is, from one point of view, an altogether human book written by fallible human beings; yet God speaks through their words as they bear witness to him. It is not necessary, therefore, to regard every word in the Bible as accurate or absolutely correct in every sense. The Bible is not a textbook in geography or science or ordinary history. It is testimony literature and must be read as such throughout. The biblical writers were children of their times and were mistaken about many things about which we today may be better informed. Yet their testimony to God and his mighty acts is faithful, true, and to be relied upon as "a lamp shining in a dark place, until the day dawns and the morning star rises" (2 Peter 1:19). "But we have this treasure in earthen vessels, to show that the transcendent power belongs to God and not to us" (2 Corinthians 4:7).

If we read and study the Bible as the Word of God in the sense we have described, we must read and study it from the center, which is always Jesus the Christ. He is the axle on which the whole wheel turns and the linchpin which keeps the wheel from spinning off.

Continuing revelation

God has not stopped revealing himself; he continues to make himself known by acting in history as he acted in those events to which the Bible witnesses. The establishment, spread of the church, and all that has happened through its two thousand year history is a self-revelation of God. However, God's continuing revelation is not limited to what goes on in the Christian church. God is the Lord of all history. He is active in all the world, guiding people to his purposes. His activity in the world is, for the most part, hidden and cannot be seen except with the eyes of faith. What we do see is determined by and understood on the basis of the testimony of the Word of God.

It should also be clear that God's continuing self-revelation is always in, through, and with people. God makes himself known through the living voice of the gospel in the mouths of people, a matter we will discuss in later chapters.

Summary statements

Below are statements to help you recall and think about some of the things you have read in this chapter.

1. People load the term god with many different meanings.

2. Where your heart is, there is your god.

3. The Lord God alone is to be worshiped and to receive our supreme allegiance.

4. God never appears to us face to face in his naked glory.

5. We fear, love, trust, and obey an unseen God.

6. The hidden God confronts us in the masks of creation, but finally and decisively in Jesus the Christ.

7. The Bible is the record of the acts of God interpreted by prophets and apostles.

8. Jesus the Christ is the Word of God.

9. God continues to make himself known by acting in today's world and in today's events.

The Hand of Blessing

"And God saw everything that he had made, and behold, it was very good."

Genesis 1:31

Chapter Two
WE BELONG TO GOD

Was the world created by God, or did it come into being through natural processes? Are science and the Bible necessarily at odds in their views of the world? What does it mean to be created in "the image of God"? What is the goal toward which the whole creation is moving?

Genesis and science

In the famous Scopes Trial of 1925, William Jennings Bryan and Clarence Darrow debated whether God created the world and human life or whether all the world was the result of material evolution. Since the trial practically all educated people have come to accept some kind of evolutionary view as the most reasonable and probable explanation of our changing world.

Nevertheless, there are still those who insist on taking the Genesis account in the Bible as literally as did William Jennings Bryan. The result is that they continue to see a conflict between a six-day creation in Genesis and the view that the world may have originated in some other manner. Others believe that the Genesis account can easily be harmonized with an evolutionary point of view. They regard the six days as six periods of God's creative activity, which began with the origin of galaxies and planets from a previously unclassified mass of energy and ended with human life as descended with the ape from a common, subhuman ancestor.

Not how but why

Still others, however, harmonize Genesis and science in quite a different way. The Bible is not a science textbook, they say. God doesn't have to reveal matters that humans can discover for themselves with their God-given brains. So the question to which biblical revelation addresses itself is not how the world came to be as it is today, but the more basic question as to why there is anything at all. Why is there something instead of nothing? This is the question that arises when we recognize we are limited in knowledge and power, and especially when we face the shock of the "why" of our own being in the world.

Cosmology or cosmogony

The Genesis account, as God's Word to us, is not to be taken either as a scientific cosmology or cosmogony. A cosmology is a reasoned picture of the cosmos or universe. A cosmogony is a theory about the origin or genesis of the cosmos.

The writers of Genesis thought of a three-storied universe: heaven, earth, and underworld (see Exodus 20:4). Today this cosmology has been so enlarged that it staggers the imagination. The speed of light is approximately 186,300 miles per second, and a light year is the distance which light travels in a year. Our nearest fixed star is about four and one-half light years away. There are stars whose light burned out at the time Christ was born, but which we can still see today because the light is just now reaching us. Beyond are galaxies upon galaxies of star systems reaching off into distances that seem to have no end. In view of this the words of the psalmist take on additional meaning: "When I look at thy heavens, the work of thy fingers, the moon and the stars which thou hast established; what is man that thou art mindful of him, and the son of man that thou dost care for him?" (Psalm 8:3–4).

The cosmogony of the Book of Genesis corresponds to but is different from other, older cosmogonies that depict God's creative work as similar to what human beings do when they make something. The Bible's point, however, is that things come into being by the power of God's creative Word. "For he [God] spoke, and it came to be; he commanded, and it stood forth" (Psalm 33:9).

Modern cosmogonies base themselves on observation of how physical particles behave and on sophisticated guesses of how things may have gotten to be as they are. Whatever the Bible has to say to us, then, must be quite independent of any cosmology or cosmogony, either ancient or modern. The biblical witness serves a purpose different from scientific explanation. The Bible does not go into detail about the "how," but witnesses to the "who" and the "why" of creation.

God made me

The essential question of creation is not what may have happened at the beginning of time, but how we view our own existence in the world today. Only after this question has been answered can the question about origins arise.

We must first ask, Do I acknowledge that I am dependent for my very being and for everything I have upon the creative power of a gracious God? Luther encouraged this kind of question in *The Small Catechism*. Instead of discussing how the world began, he fashioned his explanation of the First Article of the Apostles' Creed into a first person matter.

When I confess that "I believe in God the Father almighty, Maker of heaven and earth," I am acknowledging a very specific relation to a very specific Lord God. The implication is that I am making this confession on my knees and not just as an objective, perhaps even disinterested spectator. Because of this confession, my life is quite different from what it would have been without it. If not, I either do not know what I am saying, or I am rejecting the Lord God because of the claim he puts upon me—a claim which may offend me, hurt my pride, or shatter my trust in my own brains and powers.

Here is what Luther says: "I believe that God has created me and all that exists. He has given me and still preserves my body and soul with all their powers. He provides me with food and clothing, home and family, daily work, and all I need from day to day. God also protects me in time of danger and guards me from every evil" (*The Small Catechism*, Explanation to the First Article of the Apostles' Creed).

That is a mouthful. It means that although I know that I was born of a father and mother, as all human beings are, and although I can watch conception in a test tube, nevertheless I and all creatures finally owe existence to the creative power of God. Our existence as human beings is the result of God's creative action, not our own.

Furthermore, not only is the initial gift of life from God, so also is the continuation of life. To be sure, the whole world owes its being to God's creative fiat, "Let it be!" But the world and all that is in it would sink into nothingness if not upheld by God's creative will.

Ground of being

The universe, then, is not self-sustaining; its existence depends upon an "other" who is not a part of the universe. With this in mind theologian Paul Tillich spoke of the Creator as not one being among others, but as the "ground of all being" without whom nothing can exist. The difference between the Creator and creature is not just a matter of degree, as between a supreme being and a lesser being. It is a qualitative difference, not of degree but of kind. The gap between Creator and creature cannot be bridged by degrees any more than a daredevil might try to jump over the Grand Canyon by degrees. God is the

Creator; he alone has his being in and of himself. Everyone and everything else is creature. Our being depends at all times on the creative will of the Creator. All would sink into nothingness if God chose to withdraw his support, a fact that puts the created world into its proper place (see Isaiah 40:12–31).

The ontological shock

Either I have my life entirely of myself and can draw on it ceaselessly without the least anxiety that it should ever fail, or I experience what Paul Tillich called the "ontological shock" (the shock that affects my very being—*ontos* means "being"). Suddenly I experience the shocking realization that any moment may be my last, like the heart patient with angina pectoris who struggles desperately to get his or her breath. There is no anguish (angina) quite like that.

The ontological shock may also come to us as we watch another person die. An artery has been cut, and blood spills out onto the sand where it cannot be gathered up again. Or we stand beside the lifeless body of a loved one and look into the eyes from which the light of life has flown, and we feel absolutely helpless. Then we begin to realize what it means that we are creatures, not creators. Then we need to know the One who says "I am the resurrection and the life" and who with a word can bring life out of death.

Luther makes explicit that God is the One who supplies us with all we need for human life—the food we eat, the clothing we wear, the music in which we rejoice, our families, our homes, our automobiles, our spaceships. All these are masks behind which God is present to us, blesses us, and calls us to thankfulness. Through his presence and activity in the masks of creation, God also "protects [us] in time of danger and guards [us] from every evil."

Goodness and mercy

We now come to a most important consideration. Luther concludes his Explanation of the First Article as follows: "All this he does out of fatherly and divine goodness and mercy, though I do not deserve it. Therefore I surely ought to thank and praise, serve and obey him. This is most certainly true."

All that we are and have is God's gracious gift which we have not earned or in any way deserved. Therefore, we "surely ought to thank and praise, serve and obey him."

We do not just intellectually acknowledge that long ago a wise, powerful, and good being must have made the world. On the contrary, we acknowledge right now and at every moment how it really is with us as creatures. Moreover, we express our creature-likeness by being thankful and obedient. Only then are we confessing faith in God the Creator as he is witnessed to in the Bible.

God's creation is a work of love, as the Old Testament makes clear. Israel's deliverance from Egypt was an undeserved act of God's grace. From the vantage point of that deliverance, the Israelites looked back and saw the creation of the world as the same kind of gracious act.

Creation as God's gracious act is clear also in the New Testament. There we are told that the worlds were made by the Word of God. This Word became flesh in Jesus and lived among us "full of grace and truth," revealing God's glory (John 1:14).

Possibility of offense

The God who made, preserves, and protects us also puts a claim upon us. He asks for our thanks, praise, and trusting obedience. But someone may say: "What do you mean I owe all I am and have to this God who never shows his face? I've been around. I know how things came to be and that I'm the end product of natural forces. All the powers of my brain and body can be accounted for. And what's this folderol about owing all I possess to this invisible God! I have worked hard for what I have while others wasted their talents and starved. Certainly I am grateful for what I have, and I pay my tribute to the marvels of nature. But why should I go beyond that?

"Then there is all this malarkey about God providing for our every need and protecting us from all danger and harm! To believe that there is an all-loving Creator and Provider is just too much when you look at the world hunger situation, cancer, heart disease, and the like. If people are sick or otherwise incapacitated so that they have no hard-earned riches to share, starvation and suffering will never be brought to an end. It's up to humankind to provide as much security as possible for itself. It may be okay for a few fortunate ones to thank and serve the God who has been good to them, but what about the millions whom God has forgotten?"

Such talk may indicate proud and open rebellion at not wanting to have any Lord over you. It may also be a subtle way of glorying in one's own achievements or sufferings on behalf of less fortunate people. So the idea of God as Creator may offend those who think they are products of natural causes or who question evil in the world.

Image of God

The Bible says that humankind, male and female, were created in the "image of God" (Genesis 1:26–27). Through the years the image of God has been interpreted in different ways. Some have said it means that human beings possess a rational soul. This includes the view that the real person is a non-material soul which, unlike the body, is not subject to death and corruption. The soul enters the body at birth and leaves it again at death. The body is like a perishable house that is inhabited for a time by the incorruptible soul.

Immortal soul

The ancient Greeks clearly spelled out this view. They believed that the soul is eternal, without beginning or end, and not subject to the ravages of time, death, or decay. There never was a time when the soul was not, and there will never be a time when it will not be. Furthermore, the soul is not dependent for its being upon any creative fiat. It has its life in and out of itself, and therefore it is not dependent upon God.

There are many arguments that supposedly prove this. One such argument runs as follows: when anything in the physical world (a chair, for example, or a human body) comes into being, it does so by the accumulation of parts. A carpenter puts pieces together to make a chair. Sperm and ovum unite, are fed by other elements, and continue to divide and grow until a human body comes into being. Both the chair and the body cease to be when their pieces fall apart or decay. Some of the pieces or remaining chemical particles may go into other forms like fertilizer.

It is different with the soul. The soul is one, a unity which has no parts. It is indivisible; it cannot be subdivided. Therefore, the soul could not have come into being by the accumulation of its parts. Nor can it go out of being by falling apart since it has no parts. The soul is eternal, without beginning, without end, indestructible. It is not dependent for its being upon anything but itself.

According to ancient Greek philosophy, souls have their abode in a non-physical realm. They come from this realm and dwell in a human body for a time. After migrating from body to body for perhaps ten thousand years, they return to the realm from which they came. This makes the non-physical, non-material realm the real world, while our material world is only a shadow of the real world.

This view has had a devastating influence upon Christian belief and teaching. Regarding the material world as unreal and the non-physical, non-material realm as real has led to a deprecation of the body and to a false asceticism or other-worldliness which is quite foreign to the biblical witness. The Bible, after all, is a very earthy book whose ultimate hope is not in escape from the earth, but in the coming of a "new heaven and a new earth."

The Greek view has also led to a belief in the immortality of the soul instead of the resurrection of the entire person. In fairness to the early Christians who believed in a soul separate from the body, it must be said that they did not hold the soul to be eternal in the same sense as the Greek philosophers. Some of the early Christians believed that God had created all the souls for all future time at the very beginning. These souls were then stored in limbo and implanted one-at-a-time into individual wombs at conception. Others held that souls were traduced or transferred from parents to children at conception when a new, separate life began.

These views intended to preserve the fact that a human being is not just a body and that people cannot escape God by dying. The Bible, however, leads to a view that is more in harmony with the modern idea of the person as a psychosomatic (soul-body) unity.

Other views

Human beings, because they have the ability to think and reason, have been described as rational animals. But humans are really more than animals who think.

Humans have also been called toolmaking animals. Because of the shape of their hands, humans can juxtapose the fingers to the thumb and perform all the delicate operations of the toolmaker. On the other hand, the monkey is restricted to "monkeying around."

Humans have also been called laughing animals; they are the only beings who have the kind of physique that makes laughter possible. Hyenas, kookaburras, and other animals can make laughing noises, but they do not laugh in the sense of finding others and themselves humorous. Without a sense of humor we cease to be human and god-like. Perhaps, however, we do not know how much of a sense of humor our dog really has when he or she puts up with human behavior. Unless we have other criteria, therefore, we will not arrive at what constitutes the image of God in persons.

Humans have also been called animals who bury their dead. This may bring us closer to what is meant by the image of God since our burial customs signal our insatiable hunger for life. We think we were not made to die. When our loved ones die, we treat their remains with reverence. We have a reverence for the human body that we do not accord to the animals which provide us with food. Whether human beings bury their dead in the ground, burn them on funeral pyres, or expose them to the sun and vultures, somehow the life that was there must be returned to the place from which it came. There is talk, consequently, of an afterlife. But even this is not sufficient to explain the image of God in persons.

Image in the Bible

The Bible says that God created human beings in the image of God. The Hebrew words for image, *tselem* and *demuth*, refer to a physical image or likeness. It is not unlikely, then, that the biblical writers actually thought of humans as created in the physical image of God.

But what did this mean to them? *Tselem* and *demuth* were used to designate the images that an emperor might set up in lands over which he ruled, indicating he was lord over that area. Likewise, human beings bear God's image as they stand upon the earth, indicating that they are rulers over the creation yet always responsible to God. According to the Bible, humans are not to plunder the earth, but to till it, develop it, and to answer to God for their stewardship.

Rather than specifying a characteristic that constitutes the image of God in a person, it is therefore more in line with the biblical witness to regard persons in their totality as reflecting who and what God is.

Responsible to God

Human beings are creatures who are responsible to God. This means human beings in their totality, for they cannot be divided into bodies on the one hand and souls on the other. When the Bible says that God formed Adam out of dust from the ground and breathed into his nostrils the breath of life, this should not be interpreted to mean that he, at that point, implanted a separate soul into Adam. Instead, when God breathed upon this human creature, whose body consisted of nothing but chemical elements (mostly water and, at present inflation prices, not worth much more than a few dollars), then that body became alive; it "became a living being" (Genesis 2:7).

The Bible makes clear that human beings do not have life in and of themselves, but owe their existence at all times to God. Life is in the breath and, without God supplying breath, a person cannot live. It is as if God keeps giving mouth-to-mouth resuscitation to all living creatures; when he ceases to supply them with breath they die (see Psalm 90:3—"Thou turnest man back to the dust, and sayest, 'Turn back, O children of men!' "). Therefore, persons in their totality stand over against God as dependent creatures responsible to him.

Responsible and answerable

Human beings are creatures God can address and who must answer that word of address. They are not things which God pushes around or animals more or less safely guided by instinct. People are responsible human beings. The word *response* comes from the Latin *spons*, meaning "free will." To be responsible means to be able to respond freely out of ourselves to the word or address of another responsible being. It means being able to say yes or no without coercion to a claim made upon one's life by another.

This may be more clearly expressed in the German word *Verantwortlichkeit*, which contains the word *antwort* or "answer." Literally the word means "answer-ability," that is, the ability to answer. God asked Adam, "Where are you?" (Genesis 3:9), and Adam had to answer. God said to Cain, "Where is Abel your brother? . . . The voice of your brother's blood is crying to me from the ground." Cain answered with a refusal to be held responsible: "Am I my brother's keeper?" (Genesis 4:9–10). The risen Lord asked Peter, "Do you love me?" Peter answered, "Lord, you know everything; you know that I love you." The Lord said, "Feed my sheep" (John 21:17).

God, therefore, created the kind of being with whom he could have, in Martin Buber's terms, an *I–Thou* rather than an *I–It* relationship. An I–It relationship is one in which the I manipulates the It, pushing the It around as the I pleases. An I–Thou relationship is one in which the I fully respects the freedom and integrity of the Thou, drawing that person with cords of love—as the Lord God drew the people of Israel (Hosea 11:4), as Hosea drew back his adulterous wife (Hosea 3:1–5), and as the waiting father drew the prodigal home (Luke 15:11–32).

Finite or limited freedom

We have said that the human being's ability to respond to another being implies free will. This freedom, however, needs qualification. People are by no means free as God is. As creatures, they are decidedly limited or finite. They are limited in time and space, in knowledge, and in power. There are many factors in life over which they have ab-solutely no control. They do not choose their own fathers and mothers; they have a definite heredity and are born into a specific environment. They are, as the existentialist philosophers say, spit into existence like a spot on the wall, without being asked why or where, and are subjected to incalculable and ridiculous turns of fate.

One of the paradoxes of human life, then, is destiny and freedom, or simultaneously not being free and being free. Being free but not absolutely free is the person's glory, but also his or her undoing. Freedom is the basis of human creativity and mastery over nature. But it is also the basis of people's overreaching themselves in pride or, on the other hand, of not living up to their potential.

Complete determinism

The analogy of a train running along tracks that stretch endlessly in both directions helps clarify the predicament of limited or finite freedom. Think of this train as having a number of windowless box cars filled with all kinds of items. These windowless cars and their contents are being dragged along without any choice or knowledge of where they are going and why. There is no freedom whatsoever in this situation, only what some have called complete determinism. It could be that people are boxed in in a similar way, completely determined by factors over which they have no control even though they may think otherwise.

The freedom of God

Now think of a being completely outside the train, a model train-builder who built the train and controls it. This being is completely outside the endless tracks of space and time and, in fact, in another dimension. He knows the source of the tracks and where they lead because he is their creator. He is not himself caught up in the limitations of space and time, but surveys them from his lofty heights like an eagle soaring over the highest mountain tops.

If there are any limitations upon an all-powerful, creative "ground of all being," they are self-imposed. The greatest show of omnipotence is withholding one's power in order not to destroy the measure of freedom granted the creature. This is the kind of omnipotence God himself shows who, when he limits the exercise of his power, has no anxiety because he is still always in complete control. Human beings with their limited freedom, lack this power and, consequently, destroy those they love. For example, think of parents who will not cut the umbilical cord or totalitarian dictators who sacrifice millions to bring about their utopias.

The engineer

Where do human beings fit in this analogy? They are neither completely determined like the contents of the box car, nor are they like God in his sovereign freedom. Rather, they are like the engineer in the old song who mounts "to the cabin with his orders in his hands." Human beings are clearly limited in what they can know and do. The train was there before they boarded it, so they are not certain of its origin. Also, they cannot look all the way back along the tracks, and there is always another bend around which they cannot see. Human beings cannot see the beginning of time (a contradictory expression since we experience time as a time before which there is more time), nor can they see ahead to where the tracks will lead. Therefore, they can never know just what the future holds for them.

But the engineer does know where he boarded the train. Also, he has his orders in his hand, knows where he is supposed to take the train, and is aware of what he must do to get it there on time. There are rules for all that. He cannot make the train take off and fly across the mountains as a shortcut. Besides, there are all kinds of contingencies he cannot completely control—a cow on the tracks, an open switch, a failure of power. So his journey is fraught with a kind of anxiety that neither God nor the completely determined being share.

The engineer is not just concerned about himself. He is responsible also for the precious cargo he carries, all those travelers who are depending upon him to take them safely to some eagerly anticipated rendezvous or back home to the bosom of their families. What a burden of responsibility! Besides that, he never knows when time will run out for him. And what then? Ah, there's the rub! In Shakespeare's words, "To be, or not to be: that is the question."

Anxiety or dread

From the moment life begins in the precarious shelter of the womb until life ends, people are insecure in their finite freedom. They are free, but not absolutely free; they are in control of their destiny, but only partially so. So all their lives are fraught with anxiety or dread.

Anxiety is to be distinguished from fear. Fear is being afraid of a definite object. Most fears are learned because of something that has frightened us. It's different with anxiety or dread, the necessary and constant concomitants of our limited freedom. Anxiety is like an organ pedal that becomes stuck and drones on no matter what other music we play, even if we momentarily are not conscious of the stuck pedal. The anxiety of our finite freedom is the state out of which comes both our creativity and our sin. Because we are insecure we try to increase our power over our environment and, in so doing, we tragically overstep our limitations, plunder the planet, and destroy our fellow humans.

Material image

We have been discussing what has been called "the formal image of God," that is, the form a person possesses to be capable of communion with God and the limitations of that form. We have not made any references to the content or material poured into that form ("the material image of God"). What is the content poured into the form? If persons are created in God's image, they must in some way reflect what God is like. If God is trustworthy and fair, his creatures must also be trustworthy and fair. If God is love, people must reflect that love.

Persons and their relations

Since persons are not the authors of their own existence, the term "image of God" is particularly appropriate. We cannot really point to a single, stable quality that constitutes the image of God in persons. Here, however, modern science may help us.

At one time scientists thought the universe consisted of atoms, that is, of irreducible, tiny pellets of solid matter that bounced around like pool balls on a table. These atoms, it was believed, were energized from within or pushed around by exterior forces (giant cue sticks in giant hands). Now we know better. The atom has been split, and we know that nothing is stable in and of itself. Everything depends for its stability upon the relations in which it exists.

So it is with people. They are always persons-in-relation to themselves, to their environment, to other human beings, to the whole universe, to the farthest star. Everything is interrelated, so much so that we do not know what effect an intergalactic event might have on our planet and on us. If the whole universe is dependent upon God, then humankind's relation to God is crucial. People cannot maintain their equilibrium or stability unless they are properly grounded in a trusting relationship with the God who is the source of their lives.

The so-called "material image of God" depends upon relationships. To change the picture somewhat, think of the moon. It has no light of its own, but reflects the light of the sun. How much light it reflects depends upon how we see it in relation to the source of light. It may be seen as only a slender sickle or the glorious full moon.

Likewise, persons can reflect God's love only if the relationship to the source of love is right and to the degree that there is no obstruction in the way. Human beings were created to live in a relationship of trust in the Lord God and to become the clear channel of that love to others. "We love, because he first loved us" (1 John 4:19).

Jesus was rightly related to the Father and, consequently, clearly reflected the fulness of God. He truly bore the image of God (Colossians 1:15). Since we know God fully only in Jesus the Christ, it is to him we must be related in trust. "And we all, with unveiled face, beholding the glory of the Lord, are being changed into his likeness from one degree of glory to another; for this comes from the Lord who is the Spirit" (2 Corinthians 3:18; see also Colossians 3:10; Ephesians 4:23–24).

Male and female

Among the most profound words in the Bible are those concerning humankind's creation in God's image: "Male and female he created them" (Genesis 1:27). From the beginning the human race existed as male and female.

The biblical creation story differs decidedly from the Greek story of creation. The latter posits an original being which combined both male and female genders, and which was then split in two. Ever since, the two have been trying to get together again. This would imply that neither man nor woman is a complete individual without the other.

The Bible presents us with a different picture. Each person, Eve as well as Adam, is an individual in her or his own right from the very start. The God-relation is strictly an *individual* relationship with a person. God addresses not crowds, but individual responsible beings by name. Each person must answer for herself or himself.

Yet there is really no individual except the individual-in-community. Being fully human is impossible in lonely isolation. Persons cannot be aware of or know themselves except in relation to others.

Furthermore, all people are created equal before the law, in God's sight, and in dignity. All are created equally in God's image, equally responsible, and equally beloved. Yet all people are not the same like peas in a pod. This is not only indicated by the startling fact that the fingerprints of no two individuals are alike, but also by peoples' great variety of talents, capacities, looks, colors, shapes, and the like. Such variety makes for cooperative community. Imagine the lack of ability and cooperation in a football team consisting of nothing but 300-pound tackles or 150-pound running backs.

The goodness of sex

A basic, ineradicable difference between persons is the sexual one upon which the continuance of the human race, the family, the school, and the community depend. "And God saw everything that he had made, and behold, it was very good" (Genesis 1:31). So the male-female relationship was also good.

A strange anomaly is the development of many taboos and fears connected with sex. Nevertheless, it is not at all reprehensible that in all cultures restraints have been placed upon the exercise of this impetuous urge. It is altogether strange, however, that sexual intercourse should have come to be regarded as intrinsically evil and virginity as a high virtue. Sexual intercourse presumably transmitted sin; therefore, to some minds, Mary had to be immaculately conceived, and Jesus had to be born of a virgin.

On the other side, the openness of sex has been effectively championed in recent years, resulting in all the license and perversity that characterize much of today's sexual liberation.

God's continuing creation

We have indicated several times that the created world is not unreal or evil and that salvation does not consist of escaping from it. Rather, the God who created the world is also the Guarantor of its fulfillment. This idea will receive fuller treatment in the last chapter, but should not just be tacked on at the end. The consummation of all things must be present from the start and must be part of our thinking at all times. We therefore conclude this chapter with a quotation from the letter to the Ephesians: "For God has allowed us to know the secret of his plan, and it is this: he purposes in his sovereign will that all human history shall be consummated in Christ, that everything that exists in Heaven or earth shall find its perfection and fulfillment in him. And here is the staggering thing—that in all which will one day belong to him we have been promised a share" (Ephesians 1:9–12, *The New Testament in Modern English* by J. B. Phillips).

Summary statements

Here are eleven statements to help you recall some of what you have read in this chapter.

1. The Bible emphasizes the "who" and the "why" of creation.

2. The world and all that is in it would sink into nothingness were it not upheld by God's creative will.

3. God supplies us with all that we need for human life, even though we have not earned or in any way deserve his gracious gifts.

4. The God who made, preserves, and protects us asks for our thanks, praise, and trusting obedience.

5. The "image of God" is a way of saying that human beings in their totality were made to reflect who and what God is.

6. There is a qualitative difference between the Creator and the creature.

7. Even though human beings have been created in God's image, they are nevertheless limited in what they can know and do.

8. Human beings were created to live in a trust relationship with God and to be channels of his love in the world.

9. Male and female have been created equally in God's image.

10. The male-female relationship and its expression in sexual intercourse is part and parcel of God's good creation.

11. All human history and everything that exists in heaven and earth will find its perfection and fulfillment in Christ.

Temptation and Fall

"Did God say, 'You shall not eat . . . ?' "

Genesis 3:1

Chapter Three
SIN CORRUPTS GOD'S CREATION

Why is there evil, wrong, and suffering in the world? What is sin and who is responsible for it? Are all creatures sinners? How does sin manifest itself in human beings? Are all humans created sinful? Is there any hope for this sin-corrupted world?

In the previous chapter we said that the world belongs to God who in love made us all creatures. We also said that he still preserves us and the world, and supplies us and all creatures with everything we need for life. This is God's world. He has not abdicated as its Lord God. He will finally bring this world to the fulfillment he envisioned for it from the beginning.

But what a sorry contradiction our actual world with all its evil and suffering is to this idealistic picture! We therefore face what is intellectually, emotionally, and existentially a most difficult problem.

Evil and suffering

We have dealt with the question, Why is there something and not nothing? Now we must ask why this something that is so beautiful and fulfilling is also so ugly and destructive.

Some say, perhaps naively, that all the evil, wrong, and suffering in the world exist because we have not evolved sufficiently. The age of our earth has been estimated as four and one-half billion years. Given the billions of years of the evolutionary process, we today are living only in the dawn of conscience.

If you represent this span of time by the twenty-four hour movement of the hands of a clock from noon until noon, then 10:51 A.M. marks the awakening of organic life; twenty-two seconds before noon marks the appearance of human life; and the whole of recorded world history will have transpired in the last three-tenths of a second.

Furthermore, the beginning of natural science actually dates from about A.D. 1600. But it has not been until the present generation that such amazing advances have been made as the splitting of the atom, which marked the beginning of the space age. Think of what an infinitesimal fraction of time this represents on the cosmic clock.

So, you might ask, why all this pessimism about the world going to the dogs? Just give us time. The real problem is our ignorance and our culture's lagging behind the breakthroughs of science. After all, if it's only less than one and one-half hours since life emerged out of the swamps and only a few seconds since human beings got down out of the trees, we really have nothing to be pessimistic about.

Such an attitude, however, has a strangely naive ring about it in a century that has witnessed the unspeakable horror of two world wars and presently lives under the mushroom cloud of nuclear destruction. In addition, this century has experienced the near dissolution of western culture and the deep anguish of many people who have lost their moorings and have become like sheep without a shepherd. What comfort is it to the people of this century that, given a few more million years, things will supposedly get better? What concerns people today is the mess in which we presently find ourselves. Why are things in such a mess?

Sin in the Bible

The Bible talks about the presence of evil in the world stemming from peoples' abuse of the prerogatives and limitations of their creaturehood. The human condition is such that people are free, but not absolutely free. On the one hand, persons pridefully exceed their limitations. On the other, in weakness and sloth, they fail to live up to the great possibilities open to them. This is what the Bible calls sin in contrast with what we ordinarily regard as sin.

Whatever became of sin

The well-known psychoanalyst Karl Menninger has publicized the word *sin* in a book with the intriguing title *Whatever Became of Sin?* People still use the word sin and many of the other great words of the Christian vocabulary. But what does the word really mean? As with other words, sin has lost its specific Christian meaning for many people.

The idea of sin has been either utterly trivialized or derided as an old-fogyish, killjoy notion that no self-respecting twentieth century person can tolerate. It is regarded as any breach of what the cultural majority considers decent, from breaking the rules of etiquette and health to breaking the ritual observances of church and synagogue. It's a sin to use foul language, to smoke, to wear or not to wear certain clothes, to eat certain foods on certain days, to do certain things on the Sabbath. Sin is also equated with the repression of healthy appetites and urges. According to some people, everything that is fun or fattening is a sin. Moreover, for many people the word sin suggests sexual impulses and all the taboos connected with sex. The notion of sin, they say, also leads to false guilt feelings. So the sooner you get rid of the whole murky mess of sin and guilt the better.

Instead of sin for which we are responsible, for which we must repent, and for which we need forgiveness, we have

ignorance or weakness. Sin is not sin, but a malfunc-
tioning of the glands or environmental effects from bad
toilet-training or a possessive father- or mother-in-law.
Always there is some cause, like a virus that produces
disease; if only we can isolate the cause, then we can cure
the malady.

What makes this situation terribly complex and difficult
is that in this age of scientific progress, much human
behavior once regarded as willfully perverse and sinful is
no longer regarded that way at all. Today such behavior is
often characterized as an illness with an identifiable cause.
Application of the right kind of therapy, then, can in many
instances cure the illness or behavior problem.

An implication that can be drawn from this modern
view is that we are not really responsible for the way we
are. Instead, we are essentially products of hereditary,
environmental, or biological factors.

The Bible, however, claims that human beings are
indeed responsible, accountable beings. We are not
merely victims of fate or of forces beyond our control. To
be human in biblical terms is to have the freedom to be
self-consciously involved in dealing with ourselves and
with those things we cannot control.

Broken relationships

In preceding sections we have been trying to make clear
that there are sinners only where there are human beings.
Human beings are not just driven by instinct, nor are they
merely victims of forces beyond their control. In addition,
human beings always live in relationships. We will
therefore have to view sin in terms of relationships. For in
the final analysis sin is a matter of broken relationships
with God, one's self, one's neighbor, and the whole created
world.

If people owe everything they are and have to the Lord
God, then their relationship with God should be in order.

Trust, thankfulness, and obedience will all be involved in a right relationship with God.

Since God is love, a person created in God's image can reflect that love as the moon reflects the light of the sun only if the relationship with God is right and unobstructed. Also, only when the relationship with God is right can persons be in the right relationship with themselves. In addition, they must be in the right relationship with God so that the love that comes from him may flow through them to their neighbors. Finally, they must be in the right relationship with God if they are not to plunder the earth, but to care for it properly.

God created people in his image so that they might take their lives from him in obedience and trust and become clear clannels of his love to others and to the world. Sin is that state or condition in which this right relationship with God is broken and, consequently, also the right relationships with one's self, one's neighbor, and the created world. Then life together in faith and in love becomes impossible.

Origin of sin

Genesis 3 tells how sin entered the world through broken relationships. Details of this story, however, should not be taken literally, as if there were an actual garden where Adam and Eve once lived in face-to-face fellowship with God who came to visit them in the cool of the day. If Adam and Eve had lived in face-to-face fellowship with God, they could not have been our progenitors; they could not have been one of us. Being human is being unable to see God in his naked glory; it is having to worship and trust an unseen God. To be human means to live by faith and not by sight. If Adam's and Eve's story is the common human story, then they too must have lived by faith and not by sight. They too must have trusted an unseen and unseeable God, taken him at his word, and believed his promises. Understood this way, the biblical story of the Fall tells the common human story of how sin enters the world through broken relationships.

Luther, however, took the Genesis 3 story literally. He supposed that it must have been morning when Adam and Eve were created. God set them down in a paradise where they could have all their needs fulfilled and even have access to eternity through the tree of life. But alas, this paradise didn't last. Hardly had the sun passed its zenith that Adam and Eve lost their paradise. Before the sun set they were driven out, and an angel with a flaming sword was sent to guard the tree of life lest people would live forever on the earth. The supposed idyllic state of integrity, wholeness, or innocence was of mighty short duration, hardly long enough for Adam and Eve to give it a try.

The first human beings lived under the same human conditions as we do. Instead of triumphing over these conditions, they succumbed to them. This means that from the beginning, human beings became sinners. They lost the state of integrity in which they might have lived. God did not create them sinners; they became sinners under the conditions of finitude, under the limitations of their creaturehood. God, therefore, cannot be blamed as the creator of sin. The human race must shoulder full responsibility for its fall. Humans did not have to sin; they had the freedom not to sin. But once they had sinned, the relationships between God and people were altered for all time.

All persons are sinners

Henceforth all people are sinners and under God's judgment. There is no way of resigning from our sinful involvement or heritage. Sinners can only beget sinners. In the Bible, for example, the first human brother who repudiated being his brother's keeper became a murderer.

Not long after, human beings in their pride attempted to build a tower high enough to dethrone God, to make a name for themselves upon the earth, and to achieve unity and peace without a God above them. But it didn't work.

Creatures who did not fall

There are other created beings who did not succumb to the conditions of their creaturehood. These creatures stand in the presence of God, surround his throne, sing his praise, and fly to do his bidding (see Isaiah 6). Again we should not be overly literal in our understanding of these creatures, the "angels." Instead, we may regard them as effective symbols of what it means to be a creature of God in full face-to-face vision of his glory, constantly lauding and magnifying his holy name and joyfully doing his bidding.

What this tells us is that we cannot equate creaturely limits with sin. Being finite does not automatically make us sinners. Creatures, as the angels illustrate, *can* recognize their creatureliness and serve God fully.

There are, then, powers in the universe that serve God and see that his will is accomplished. These "angels" have been regarded as God's messengers and instruments of his providence. Without them the future God has in store for us would be radically diminished.

Sin and the world

God set Adam and Eve in a garden and gave them permission to eat of all of its trees, including the tree of life. However, he forbade them to eat of the tree of the knowledge of good and evil: "For in the day that you eat of it you shall die" (Genesis 2:17).

This symbolizes the human condition of finite freedom. God has set us in the garden of this world. He offers us the possibility of an abundant life which, in its nature, would have no end. But there are limits; there are prohibitions ("Thou shalt nots") for our own good.

Knowledge of good and evil

If we look at the Bible's message in its entirety, we will be able to find great significance in God's command not to eat of "the tree of the knowledge of good and evil" and thereby lose access to "the tree of life." To eat of the tree of the knowledge of good and evil would mean that we ourselves become the final judges of what is good. When we decide for ourselves what is good, we come to know also what is evil. A creature who is fully subservient to God, however, would not know evil. Therefore, the knowledge of good and evil is not, as some suggest, a step up toward moral behavior, but a loss of conformity to the good.

The Tempter or Evil One, a fallen creature who opposes God's will, suggests otherwise. To disobey God, to eat of the forbidden fruit, and to make yourself a law unto yourself, he says, will not be a fall but an elevation. "You will not die. For God knows that when you eat of it your eyes will be opened, and you will be like God, knowing good and evil" (Genesis 3:4–5). There you have it! Once people decide to be their own god and determine for themselves what is good and what is evil, they have by their autonomy brought forth evil.

Human beings, then, are to live in the marvelous garden of this world under the Lord God. They must live within the limitations of their creaturehood subject not to a supreme being of their own creation, but to the Lord God who has revealed himself to Moses and the prophets. This means trusting God.

To put it bluntly, if God says something is for our good, we must believe, trust, and obey. We must not say, "You are inhibiting us. You are not seeking our good, but your own aggrandizement. You are throwing your weight around and lording it over us instead of letting us be ourselves."

Let me use a simple analogy. Phil has been left in charge of a candy store. He has been told that he may eat only a limited number of all the luscious pieces of candy that surround him. "I warn you, if you eat more, you'll end up with a terrible stomachache," says the owner. The owner goes out, leaving Phil there in the middle of all the tempting candies. The kindly storekeeper did not put Phil in the middle of all those tempting dainties and say, "Don't you dare touch any of them." Instead, he gave him freedom to enjoy the candy, but within limits for his own good.

As in the garden, however, the Tempter asks, "Did the owner really put you in here and tell you not to touch any of these goodies?" Phil knew the answer just as Eve did. Therefore, we can't say that Phil or Eve made a mistake out of ignorance. But the Tempter persists. "Why should you believe what the owner said? How does he know what your stomach can hold? He's not concerned about you, only about his cash register; he's afraid you'll eat up all his profits." So in mistrust and selfishness Phil gobbles up all he can hold. Then, when he does get his stomachache, he tries to blame his condition on someone else, even the store's owner.

The point of this analogy is that we tend to doubt and become mistrustful when limitations are placed on our freedom.

The self

Sin involves the self, the center of responsibility that we name when we say "I." The self does not come into being by itself, but is grounded in another. In other words we can know ourselves for what we are only as we trust in the God upon whom we are dependent.

58

Defiance and pride

Sin manifests itself through the self in two forms. The first is when the self exceeds its limitations, tears itself loose from its ground, and strives in defiance and pride to live as if it were not dependent upon another.

Pride can therefore be designated as the root of sin. Such pride is much more than being snooty and looking down on others, although some of this is involved. Pride can even appear under the guise of humility as shown in the story of the man who thanked God that he was not like the self-righteous Pharisee (see Luke 18:9–14).

Sin is the proud determination not to have anyone over you, to be a law unto yourself, to be God in the sense of absolute ruler. Then, when this fails, you turn against the true Sovereign and seek to destroy God and all his works. This is consummate evil, the worship of and delight in destructiveness, divisiveness, and inflicting pain and suffering. The Evil One or Satan symbolizes this kind of proud determination.

This kind of pride stands behind the Fall into sin of Adam, Eve, and all people. Sin is basically unbelief or a lack of trust rooted in pride.

Surrender and sloth

In addition to defiance and rebellion against restrictions, sin also takes the form of surrender, sloth, and not living up to our God-given potential. We can readily see how people get too big for their britches. But how about their failure to fill out those britches and become the kinds of persons they are intended to be! Kierkegaard described the sinner as one who has a house with an upper floor that is open to the light, the sun, and the stars, but who chooses to live in the cellar. Sinners are people who are content to grovel in the things of the earth and the paltry, fleeting satisfactions they offer, even though enduring satisfactions are available to them in their own house.

If people took God at his word, their potential and their relationships to other selves and the world could develop. Because of surrender and sloth, however, the good that might develop through the use of their own highest gifts never happens. Moreover, the riches of the earth are not developed in the right way, but are unused or used for less than intended. This too is sin.

Without fear of God

The *Augsburg Confession*, Article II, speaks of sin in still another way. It says that all members of the human race "are without fear of God, are without trust in God, and are concupiscent."

To fear God means to stand in awe of him to whom we owe supreme allegiance. Such fear is impossible unless we first recognize that we are under a just condemnation and deserve punishment. Recall how one criminal on the cross said to the other: "Do you not fear God, since you are under the same sentence of condemnation? And we indeed justly; for we are receiving the due reward of our deeds; but this man [Jesus] has done nothing wrong" (Luke 23:40–41).

However, we often fear all kinds of wrong things, what others might say about us, the jeers of our peers, the tyrant's blows. Jesus said, "Do not fear those who kill the body but cannot kill the soul; rather fear him [and that means God, not the Devil!] who can destroy both soul and body in hell" (Matthew 10:28). On the other hand "perfect love casts out fear" (1 John 4:18)—not just our false fears, but also the fear of God's wrath. For God in his love turns away his wrath so that we can flee from the wrathful God to the gracious God in Jesus Christ our Lord.

Concupiscence

We have previously talked about sin as a lack of trust in God. That leaves us, then, with the *Augsburg Confession's* reference to concupiscence. This unusual word (pro-nounced kahn KYOO puh sense) literally means "to desire earnestly" or "to desire inordinately." Unfortunately, the word has been associated almost exclusively with the urgency of sexual desire. But it should be understood more broadly than that as, for example, Genesis 3:6: "So when the woman saw that the tree was good for food, and that it was a delight to the eyes, and that the tree was to be desired to make one wise, she took of its fruit and ate."

In one sense, then, we can define sin as sensuality. This word also has been understood primarily in relation to sexual activity. Sensuality, however, really means seeking satisfaction in whatever gratifies the senses. It means an inordinate desire and search for satisfaction in any changeable or mutable good even if it is music or sculpture or whatever we regard as the height of sophisticated pleasure.

We must be careful here not to fall into the trap of regarding all sensual satisfaction as sin. This is often the common conception of sin: everything that gratifies the senses and gives pleasure is sin. We have tried to guard against this by speaking of *inordinate* desire, but even this is not enough.

Self-centeredness

Luther spoke of people being curved in upon them-selves, seeking themselves in everything they do or believe. Instead of being upright or righteous, standing up straight with our faces lifted toward God in trust and our hands reaching out in love to our neighbor, we have a disastrous curvature of the spine that causes us constantly to contemplate our own navels. This self-centeredness is sin since it is only in losing our lives that we will find life. Even the hedonists, who regarded pleasure as the highest good, recognized this. They said that those who directly seek pleasure will never find it. Pleasure is a by-product of absorption into something else. Those who seek themselves in all they do are incapable of self-giving love and of self-fulfillment.

Love of self is often defended as the basis of love for others. Those who do not love themselves, it is said, cannot love others. This, however, is a disastrous misuse of the word *love*. To be sure, persons must have the proper estimate of themselves in the sight of God, who values them for what they are. They should not, therefore, efface themselves, but strive to realize their potential. Only then can they really love and serve their neighbor. But this is a far cry from the self-centeredness or love of self which is sin.

Original sin

One of the most misunderstood and yet most crucial notions in Christian theology is original sin. Simply stated, this has been understood to mean that since Adam and Eve were our first parents and committed the first sin, everyone else has inherited their sinful nature. Because propagation takes place through sexual intercourse, the sexual act has been regarded as sinful. In fact, it is assumed by some that in the absence of sexual intercourse there would be no transmission of original or hereditary sin.

This becomes very misleading, given our present knowledge of heredity. Moreover, this is not what our predecessors meant when they said in the *New England Primer*, "In Adam's fall we sinned all," or when they spoke of the heritage of sin. We cannot speak of sin-genes inherited from our parents, as if our genes caused us to be born sinful in the same way that we might inherit a disease.

We have spoken differently of the origin of sin. We have said that Adam's story is the common human story. If we ask how sin came into the world, each of us must say:

"Through me. I am not the first human being, but I recognize that I am born of parents who have already sinned and that I am a part of a sinful humanity with which I must identify."

If I go back in my own life, I cannot find the point when I became a sinner. As far as I can remember I have always been a sinner. So it is as we go back into the history of the human race. We cannot find a time when humankind was not already in a broken relationship with God. This obviously leaves a heritage of woeful consequences just as my own life of broken relationships leaves such a heritage.

There is no way I can escape that heritage. I cannot resign from the human race. I must, therefore, willingly identify myself with all who are in the same boat with me. I must recognize our solidarity in sin, our common guilt, and that we are a lost and fallen race.

We can find analogies. I am of German parentage and cannot extricate myself from involvement with the German people, their glory and their shame. Though I was not directly involved, I cannot extricate myself from the guilt connected with Hitler and the holocaust, that fearful demonstration of sin and capitulation to the power of the Evil One. At the same time, I can take pride in what German people have accomplished and are accomplishing as human beings bearing the image of God without succumbing to the demonic cult of blood and soil.

Now I am an American citizen, and I identify with my country. My heart swells with pride as the flag of my country passes by. However, lest I be overcome by the same demonic pride that possessed the German people, I also identify with the sinfulness of my country so blatantly manifest everywhere.

So it is also with the whole human race. I am part of it; I cannot extricate myself from its glory and its shame. "In Adam's fall we sinned all." This describes our human condition. As the *Augsburg Confession* says, all people "are full of evil lust and inclinations from their mother's wombs."

Summary statements

Below are a number of summary statements to help you recall and think about what you have read in this chapter.

1. People are concerned about the mess in which they find themselves and their world.

2. Evil in the world stems from peoples' abuse of the prerogatives and limitations of their creaturehood.

3. Each of us is responsible for sin.

4. All people are sinners and under God's judgment.

5. Sin consists of broken relationships with God, one's self, others, and the world.

6. Sin is being curved in upon oneself, seeking the self in everything that is done or believed.

7. Original sin is, in one sense, inherited sin.

8. Sin is breaking God's law, the law of love.

9. Sinners flee for refuge to a gracious God in Jesus Christ.

The Lamb of God and Banner of Victory

"Behold, the Lamb of God, who takes away the sin of the world!"

John 1:29

Chapter Four
GOD MAKES THINGS NEW IN CHRIST

Who is Jesus? Why is he necessary? Is he fully human or more than human? What is the meaning and significance of his incarnation? His atonement? His resurrection? How are all things made new in Jesus the Christ?

As human beings and creatures of the earth, we worship and trust an unseen God. This unseen God is not far away, but actually confronts us in the masks of creation, calling us to thankful obedience. Nevertheless, we humans choose to worship the creature rather than the Creator and must bear the consequences of this disobedience. The wrong relationship with God resulting from our disobedience is the sin in which humankind has been involved from the beginning. But God did not abandon us. He chose a particular people among whom to reveal himself as our Savior and Deliverer.

Old Testament prophecy

The Old Testament contains many prophecies about the coming of One who would bring deliverance to Israel and to the whole world. These prophecies clearly state that the coming Messiah (a Hebrew word meaning "the Anointed One"; the Greek word for Messiah is "Christ") would be born of the house and lineage of David. Furthermore, the Messiah's coming would be regarded as the coming of God himself. The New Testament maintains that these lines of prophecy met and found their fulfillment in Jesus. For example, the writers of the Gospels frequently comment that "all this took place to fulfill what the Lord had spoken by the prophet" (Matthew 1:22).

The coming of Jesus in fulfillment of ancient prophecy was not obvious to everyone. Most of the Jews in Jesus' day, for example, did not think of him as the fulfillment of prophecy; nor do today's Jews. Ancient prophecy was not like a prediction whose correctness could be verified when the time came.

Old Testament prophets were persons who spoke for God. They explained what was happening and why, and they talked about what would happen in the future in a way that was not obvious to all. When a prophecy was fulfilled, the fulfillment itself clarified the prophecy. The fulfillment of the Old Testament prophecies concerning Jesus was like that. Besides clarifying these prophecies, Jesus' fulfillment of them radically corrected the nature of messianic expectations. In the end, then, Jesus could be recognized as the Messiah, the one who was to come (Matthew 11:1–6), only with the eyes of faith.

Was the Messiah to be a warlord who, as the Zealots expected, would throw off the hated yoke of Roman oppression? Or was he to be the one who would fulfill every jot and tittle of the law, as the Pharisees believed? Or was he the one who would deliberately go up to Jerusalem to suffer, die, and give his life as a ransom for many?

Correction and fulfillment

The ancient prophecies had to be clarified and corrected by their fulfillment. Moreover, the Old

Testament concept of the Lord God had to be corrected so that he could be understood as "the deliverer God" in Jesus Christ. The story of Jesus in the New Testament does this.

If we think that God in the Old Testament is exclusively a God of law who metes out rewards and punishments in strict justice, we are simply wrong and have not paid attention to the record. If we think he is a vengeful God, not a God of love, we are even more misguided. The Lord God of the Old Testament—the God of Abraham, Isaac, and Jacob—is the same as the Father of our Lord Jesus Christ. He is the God whom John described as "love" (1 John 4:8). He is the God of the covenant who chose his people out of love and who dwells among and with them on their earthly pilgrimage. He is the God who freely forgives (Isaiah 55:6-7) and whose mercies are new every morning (Psalm 59:16; 103:13). His love, mercy, and forgiveness are not only for those he chose to be his special instruments, but for all his children throughout the world. The promised Messiah is to be for all nations.

Yet the fulness of God's grace and his unconditional love needed to be spelled out still more clearly in the One who ate with publicans and sinners, and who finally gave his sinless life for the sins of the world. It was not only in Old Testament times that people believed they were justified by keeping the law. The apostle Paul also had to combat this notion even after Christ's death on the cross. And in spite of the preaching of the gospel for almost two thousand years, many people continue to believe that they can earn their salvation by their good deeds rather than by being freed in Jesus Christ to serve their neighbor.

Jesus and the law

In the Sermon on the Mount (Matthew 5—7; Luke 6:20-49) Jesus sharpened people's understanding of the law by showing that there is more involved than the outward keeping of its letter. For example, "You have heard that it was said to the men of old, 'You shall not kill; and whoever kills shall be liable to judgment.' But I say to you that everyone who is angry with his brother shall be liable to judgment" (Matthew 5:21–22). Or "You have heard that it was said, 'You shall love your neighbor and hate your enemy.' But I say to you, Love your enemies and pray for those who persecute you, so that you may be sons of your Father who is in heaven" (Matthew 5:43–45).

Jesus sharpened all the other commandments of Moses in a similar manner. However, he did not repudiate the basic moral laws embodied in the Ten Commandments (Matthew 5:17–18). Instead, he cut through all the intricate rules within rules which the Pharisees devised as means of keeping the law to perfection.

Jesus clearly demonstrated in his life what Paul later wrote: "Owe no one anything, except to love one another; for he who loves his neighbor has fulfilled the law. The commandments, 'You shall not commit adultery, You shall not kill, You shall not steal, You shall not covet,' and any other commandment, are summed up in this sentence, 'You shall love your neighbor as yourself.' Love does no wrong to a neighbor; therefore love is the fulfilling of the law" (Romans 13:8–10; see also 1 Corinthians 13).

Jesus' sinlessness

Jesus not only spoke of the fulfillment of the law, he actually fulfilled it. He was the Word become flesh also in the sense that he embodied the life God wants his creatures to live. Jesus therefore sensitizes us to the real nature of sin by his own sinlessness.

However, if we think of Jesus' sinlessness only in terms of never breaking ritual laws or the conventional laws of morality and piety, we will have been misled. The people called Jesus "a glutton and a drunkard" (Matthew 11:19) because he broke many of the revered laws. But in breaking them, he kept a higher law. We must therefore see his sinlessness in a different way.

Jesus' true humanity

The writer to the Hebrews said: "For we have not a high priest who is unable to sympathize with our weaknesses, but one who in every respect has been tempted as we are, yet without sin" (Hebrews 4:15). Moreover, the Incarnation means that Jesus was a genuine human being, a son of Adam who was descended from a motley progeny. Jesus was exactly what the record says, a carpenter from Nazareth. Think of any carpenter you may know, the genuineness of his or her humanity, and there you have Jesus. He was not God in disguise, like a police officer in plain clothes or a soldier in mufti. Thinking of Jesus as God in disguise is the ancient "docetic" heresy, that is, the heresy that claims Jesus only seemed to be human when, in reality, he was God. On the other hand, Jesus was not just a human being like other human beings because in him God became flesh.

We are trying here to assert the genuineness of Jesus' humanity. Someone once asked me whether Jesus had all the normal male parts. This question may appear blasphemous since we are accustomed to think of reproductive organs as associated with sinfulness. In addition, we think of Jesus as too ethereal or spiritual to possess such vulgar appendages. But all this questioner wanted to know was whether Jesus was really a human being like the rest of us. Was he subject to the same urges and drives as we? Did anger against brother, lustful thoughts, false pretenses, mistrust of God's goodness, or anxious thoughts about the morrow—matters he condemned in the Sermon on the Mount—ever arise in him? The writer to the Hebrews says that he was "in every respect . . . tempted as we are, yet without sin" (Hebrews 4:15). And Jesus himself asked, "Which of you convicts me of sin?" (John 8:46).

Whether Jesus was really human like the rest of us is a difficult question. Perhaps it is best to say simply that Jesus was subjected to the same conditions of finite freedom as we. Yet he did not succumb to these conditions. He was tempted as we to mistrust his heavenly Father. Yet he trusted him, was fully open to him, and obeyed him. Following his baptism by John (Matthew 3:13–17) in which he dedicated himself to do his Father's will even to death, the Tempter tempted him to avoid that death. But he went to that death anyway, trusting God to deliver him.

Like us, Jesus also was tempted to love only those persons who had something to offer in return. However, he resisted that temptation by loving all human beings and by giving up his life for them. He suffered willingly for and in the place of others. He used the powers he had because of his openness to God for the good of human beings, not for his own aggrandizement.

This, then, is one meaning of the Incarnation—that a fully human person might live out what it means to be in the right relationship with God, self, neighbor, and the created world. No one can any longer claim it can't be done, that it is only an ideal and never a reality. A fully human life has been lived and not in a phony way. That is why Jesus has been called the second Adam. The first Adam was tempted and sinned. The second Adam was likewise tempted, but did not sin. So the second Adam is the "new being" in and with whom the new age begins. As 2 Corinthians 5:17 says, "If any one is in Christ, he is a new creation; the old has passed away, behold, the new has come."

Jesus the pattern

Jesus did not just talk about God's demands and what it means to live in the kingdom of God where God's sovereignty is really observed, he actually exemplified all of this in his life. Therefore, he is the living pattern for our lives. We do not rigidly imitate that pattern, but conform ourselves to it. If we want to know what obedience to God's will is, we must look not only at what Jesus said and did, but at who he was—the kind of person he was, the inner motivation that determined his actions and gave him strength. As we look at Jesus we will come to know that we are indeed sinners, but that he was not. However, since Jesus was genuinely human and tempted as we, yet without sin, we will realize that we have no excuse for our condition. In the light of Jesus, the only sinless one, we recognize our true estate as "lost and condemned creatures" and begin to understand that we must look to him as Savior from our lost condition.

Embodiment of God's love

Now we have a second meaning of the Incarnation: Jesus embodies for us what God is, and "God is love" (1 John 4:8). Here the Bible uses *love* as a noun to describe God. The Bible often uses words which tell us what God does, but not as often what he is. God loves, and the Bible specifically states when and where and how.

Jesus is the love of God spelled out in actions. In Jesus, God's love is acted out in the flesh for people to see and touch and know. Jesus' acceptance of sinners as they are is God's acceptance. His spending of himself for others is God's spending of himself. His love to the utmost in his death on the cross is God's love to the utmost.

There can be no misunderstanding or distortion of the reality of God's love for us unless we have not walked with him and been touched by him. We know God's love as our lives are touched today by one in whom the love of Jesus lives.

Fulness of the Godhead

Jesus' contemporaries knew him as a human person. They therefore considered it the greatest blasphemy for him to presume to do what only God can do (see Matthew 9:1-8). However, after his resurrection and the sending of his Spirit, Jesus' followers believed that "in him the whole fulness of deity dwells bodily" (Colossians 2:9). He was the Word become flesh (John 1:14).

Divine and human

Based on the testimony of the Scriptures, the church later affirmed that two natures were united in Jesus—one fully human and one fully God. Since the beginning of the church's history, however, one nature has been emphasized at the expense of the other in alternating periods of time. Furthermore, some have asserted that Jesus was just a man—perhaps the best of men, but still only a man (recall the rock opera "Jesus Christ Superstar"). Others have spoken of him as God in disguise, God gone slumming for a day in a beggar's cloak.

Kierkegaard put it differently. He spoke of the king who gave up his throne to become a commoner for the love of a common maiden. Yet he could not divest himself totally of his kingly nature which was still manifest in his actions. The more we contemplate it, the more we feel that here we are confronted with a mystery that strikes us dumb with awe. It is a miracle of condescending love that we hold to be true, but that we understand only in the sense that we do not understand it.

The great Philippian hymn (Philippians 2:5-11) speaks of the One who, although he was in the form of God, did not cling to that as a robber clings to his booty. Instead, he gave it up, emptied himself, poured out all the glory of his godhead, and took on the form of a servant. He was, in fact, the humblest of servants; he became obedient unto death, even the death of the cross. Therefore "God has highly exalted him and bestowed on him the name which is above every name, that at the name of Jesus every knee should bow, in heaven and on earth and under the earth, and every tongue confess that Jesus Christ is Lord, to the glory of God the Father."

The absolute paradox

The divine and human natures in Christ confront us with what Kierkegaard called "the absolute paradox," that is, a contradiction we cannot resolve with our minds, but which nevertheless is the truth. Furthermore, Kierkegaard said that there is no way of becoming contemporary with this truth except in faith. Jesus' contemporaries who walked with him across the hills of Galilee, who witnessed his deeds of love and his miracles, who stood beneath his cross, and who saw him risen again, saw the glory of his godhead only with the eyes of faith. They had no advantage over us who see that glory hidden in the crucified and risen Lord with the eyes of faith.

A personal confession

Luther's Explanation of the First Article of the Apostles' Creed is a personal confession. So also is his Explanation of the Second Article. In response to the question about what Jesus as the Christ means for each of us personally, Luther says: "I believe that Jesus Christ—*true God*, Son of the Father from eternity, and *true man*, born of the Virgin Mary—*is my Lord*."

Then he goes right on with what in the German original continues as a one-sentence description of what this true God and true man did for my redemption. The point is, you cannot make an abstract assertion about who Jesus Christ is apart from what he has done for you personally.

Luther continues with his one-sentence confession (which we break into a number of sentences in English for the sake of clarity): "At great cost he has saved and redeemed me, a lost and condemned person. He has freed me from sin, death, and the power of the devil—not with silver or gold, but with his holy and precious blood and his innocent suffering and death. All this he has done that I may be his own, live under him in his kingdom, and serve him in everlasting righteousness, innocence, and blessedness, just as he is risen from the dead and lives and rules eternally. This is most certainly true."

For our salvation

This, then, brings us to the final meaning of the Incarnation. The Word did not become flesh just to show us what God is like, but to do something to save us from a plight from which we could in no way save ourselves. Throughout the church's history Jesus has been designated as Savior, Redeemer, Atoner, Reconciler, Victor. All of these words indicate that he did and still does something which he could not have done and continue to do except on the basis of what and who he actually is.

So *the* Christian confession is: "He saved me. He redeemed me. He washed away my sin." We affirm this belief again and again. In Baptism we are buried into Christ's death and raised with him. In the Lord's Supper we receive the body and blood of Christ "for the forgiveness of sin." Jesus is "the Lamb of God who takes away the sin of the world." During the entire Lenten season we reflect upon the meaning of the cross for us and the whole world. Without the suffering of the God-Man on Good Friday there is no joy of Easter morn.

The crucifix with the suffering God-Man upon it, crowned with thorns as king, is the central Christian symbol. It is true that the empty cross symbolizes the fact that Christ is risen and the victory won. But an empty cross of precious metal, emblazoned with jewels, too easily obscures the price at which our redemption was bought. This can, in turn, lead to "a theology of glory" rather than "a theology of the cross." Furthermore, it can lend itself too readily to reducing the Christian good news of an event to a timeless truth like "no victory without a cross." In this way it bypasses too easily what really happened on a specific hill called "the skull" outside a specific city wall—"crucified under Pontius Pilate."

There is no question, then, that at the center of the historic Christian faith is the cross of Christ. What happened on that cross had to do with sin and being freed from it. Jesus died for the sins of the world. How glibly we say that! But what does it mean?

Vicarious atonement

God's act in Jesus the Christ on the cross is like a diamond with many facets. All of these facets are important if the whole diamond is to shine in all of its brilliance. Similarly, not one of the many facets of the cross alone or all of them put together can exhaust the meaning of that event.

One facet concerns Jesus' bearing people's punishment, thereby freeing them from what they rightfully deserve. This facet has been described as "the vicarious atonement," a corollary to the doctrine of sin that puts a person under God's judgment. This facet is inseparable also from the conception of a God who is not just that kindly person upstairs, but who is the Holy One whose will cannot be broken with impunity or without punishment. Voltaire, the sixteenth century French writer, said scoffingly, "God will pardon. That's his business." True. But if sin is taken seriously, God's wrath and punishment must be taken with equal seriousness.

Anselm (1033–1109), archbishop of Canterbury, began his famous treatis *Cur Deus Homo* (Why did God have to become man?) by stressing the heavy burden of sin—so heavy indeed that only God is good and great enough to lift it from humanity's shoulders.

According to Anselm, God is an infinite being, and any offense against him is likewise infinite. Human beings, because of their sinfulness and their infinite offense against God, owe him an infinite debt. Because they are finite, human beings cannot possibly pay that debt. They therefore deserve infinite punishment. Unless God does something to change the situation, human beings are doomed to everlasting punishment.

Since the infinite God has been offended, he must become involved if there is to be reconciliation and atonement. Only one who is himself infinite can atone for an infinite guilt. Only an infinite God can bear an infinite punishment.

Anselm says that is why God steps in. The One who has been offended takes the punishment upon himself so that the seriousness of the offense not be minimized and so that his holiness might be vindicated at the same time his love is manifested. The finite sufferings of Jesus on the cross are the infinite sufferings of God. This really boggles the mind and rends the heart. If you add up all the pain and suffering in the world through the years—however awful that is—it is still only a finite amount. But God's suffering, like his love, is infinite and knows no limits. His suffering is for the sake of others, for their benefit as well as in their place. That is what is meant by "vicarious atonement."

Why did God have to become man? Because he alone could atone for humanity's offense. Since human beings caused the offense, God had to suffer as a human and, from that side, offer up the once-for-all and all-sufficient sacrifice. It should be remembered, however, that there is not a shred of merit attaching to sinful humans in the offering of this sacrifice. God and God alone makes the sacrifice.

Courtroom analogy

So far we have dealt with the so-called punishment aspect of the atonement. Next we will look at the justice aspect. To illustrate this we can use the courtroom analogy of the guilty prisoner who is arraigned before the judge and who can do nothing but plead his or her guilt, with no clever lawyer to find a loophole. Then, in this strange court, there is one who is the advocate and who not only speaks up for the guilty, but also takes the guilty person's punishment so that he or she may go free. As the writer of the Epistle says, "If any one does sin, we have an advocate with the Father, Jesus Christ the righteous" (1John 2:1).

Luther said we cannot stand in the presence of the righteous Judge in our own righteousness, which in God's sight is as filthy rags or a polluted garment (Isaiah 64:6). We can stand before God only in that "strange and foreign righteousness" of Christ which covers our unrighteousness.

To change the image, we read in the parable of the wedding feast: "Friends, how did you get in here without a wedding garment which I as the host was gracious enough to provide?" (a paraphrase of Matthew 22:1–11). We cannot sit at the marriage supper of the Lamb unless we let our dirty everyday dress, which has been soiled by our sins, be covered by the spotless robe the bridegroom provides.

Christ the Victor

Now let us look at the cross of Christ in still another way. This way requires the use of an analogy different from that of a court of law or a sacrifice. We have here the picture of a great struggle in which Christ emerges as the victor. This way of looking at the cross has been called the *Christus Victor* (Christ the Victor) motif.

The basic notes which run through a musical composition, giving it its peculiar quality in spite of all the variations, constitute the dominant motif of that composition. Likewise, in theology there is a dominant way of looking at the relationships between God and people that colors everything else that might be said. For example, if the dominant motif is God's love (*agape*), this will affect everything else that is said, including also what is said about the wrath of God and the law. When the God who is love uses the law, it is the left hand of the same God of love who uses the right hand to bless.

Concerning the cross of Christ, then, if the dominant motif is victory in a struggle, this puts what we have said about the "vicarious atonement" in a different light. It keeps the atonement from becoming a bargain counter transaction where the concern is more that justice should be done than that love should triumph.

That the *Christus Victor* motif is the dominant motif in Luther's "theology of the cross" is evident from his Explanation of the Second Article, which we have already discussed. There are enemies arrayed against people. These enemies include *the guilt and power of sin, the wrath of God, the curse of the law, and the power of death and the Devil.* All of these are too great for people, but Jesus the Christ wins the victory over them for us.

We have already said that one way of perceiving how persons are freed from the wrath of God is to think of God as taking the punishment upon himself. Now we are looking at the guilt and power of sin, not as an offense against God, but as enemies that rule over people and hold them in bondage. It therefore takes a real struggle to liberate people. Luther says in his Explanation of the Second Article: "At great cost he has saved and redeemed me, a lost and condemned person. He has freed me from sin, death, and the power of the devil—not with silver or gold, but with his holy and precious blood and his innocent suffering and death."

The English word *redeem* can be misleading. It can suggest buying back an article that someone has pawned, an over-the-counter transaction. This is not at all Luther's picture which, instead, suggests a prison in which people are held captive. Their freedom depends not upon the payment of a ransom, but upon a life and death struggle. "At great cost" does *not* suggest a money transaction. Freedom comes "not with silver or gold, but with his holy and precious blood and his innocent suffering and death."

The physical sufferings of Christ are sometimes morbidly dwelt on. In one sense, however, the mockery, scourging, and crucifixion to which Jesus was subjected were mild compared with the tortures people have endured (slaveships, being torn limb-from-limb, the holocaust—the list of inhuman cruelties is unbelievable!). Many crucified criminals hung on the cross for days before they finally died of thirst, starvation, heat, and exhaustion. Jesus hung there only for a few hours. Anselm therefore was right: there is more involved here than the suffering of a human person. The sufferings of Christ cannot be restricted to those last hours in Jerusalem. His whole life was one of suffering. When we contemplate all the sufferings of humankind, we must remember that God suffers in those sufferings too. When people cried out in the midst of the terrors of the holocaust "Where now is God?" Elie Wiesel pointed to the tortured victims and said, "There [in your sufferings] is God."

We should not think only of passive sufferings, where the sufferer is the victim of circumstance. Rather, the sufferings of Christ should remind us of the soldier who is engaged in battle and who must endure all the hardships of a long campaign. It takes all the soldier's strength, endurance, and wiles to cope with an enemy who is determined to win. In Jesus the Victor we are dealing with one who is engaged in a fierce struggle with the enemy.

Other Christ-figures

There have been all kinds of Christ-figures throughout the church's history, from the clown to the lord of the dance to Snoopy to the guerilla fighter struggling on behalf of the poor. Each has its measure of justification; each has a point of comparison that is legitimate, provided we do not press it beyond its limits. The clown reminds us of Paul's remarks about the foolishness of the cross (1 Corinthians 1:18–30); it was in simplicity, humility, and the combination of sadness and laughter that God walked the earth in Jesus. The lord of the dance and Snoopy remind us that Jesus attended many a feast and spread abroad true joy. Furthermore, although Jesus was not a Zealot and therefore cannot be identified with present day guerilla fighters, God may nevertheless be involved in those struggles for freedom using, as we said, his left hand to wrest power from the tyrant's hand. In this context, however, we see Jesus as the fighter who opposes a different and even more total tyranny from which people are unable to free themselves. It takes the only Invulnerable One to win this battle.

Victory over the tyrants

The guilt and power of sin are inextricably entwined with other tyrants such as the law, the wrath of God, and the power of death and the Devil.

From one point of view the law is good—if we see it as the expression of God's will for us and for our happiness in life. As Psalm 119:105 says, "Thy word is a lamp to my feet and a light to my path." From another point of view, however, the law is the greatest of tyrants because it always accuses, constantly hounds us, and never gives us rest. Always and everywhere it says "Thou shalt not" and even more devastatingly "Thou shalt." It was the law that made Paul cry out: "For I do not do the good I want, but the evil I do not want is what I do. . . . Wretched man that I am! Who will deliver me from this body of death?" (Romans 7:19; 24). Paul personifies both sin and the law as active powers.

We have already indicated that the wrath of God is one of the tyrants people must face. The guilt and power of sin and the law are so stringent because they signify living under the judgment of a holy and righteous God. The holy and righteous God says, "I am the LORD, that is my name; my glory I give to no other" (Isaiah 42:8). In denouncing the scribes and Pharisees, Jesus said: "Woe to you . . . You serpents, you brood of vipers, how are you to escape being sentenced to hell?" (Matthew 23:29; 33). When he drove the moneychangers from the Temple, Jesus said: "Depart from me, you cursed, into the eternal fire prepared for the devil and his angels" (Matthew 25:41). Only God in his love is sufficient to overcome the tyranny of this wrath.

Then there is the last enemy—death—as the wages of sin. We have talked about our subjection to death. As long as we hold to some kind of inherent life that is our own possession, the tyrant of death still has us in its grip. What we need is one who is stronger than death to break its power, one "who alone has immortality" (1 Timothy 6:16). We need someone who knows the way to go with us through that fearful dark because he himself went that way and emerged in the light that knows no dark. Every person must die his or her own death; no one can go with us into death except the One who conquered death.

Finally, there is the Devil or the Evil One. Here the struggles against the powers come to a climax, especially when we consider the power of evil in the world, which is so frightfully evident in the twentieth century. The words of the Epistle seem contemporary: "Your adversary the devil prowls around like a roaring lion, seeking some one to devour" (1 Peter 5:8). To struggle against this power we need the "whole armor of God, that [we] may be able to stand against the wiles of the devil. For we are not contending against flesh and blood, but against the principalities, against the powers, against the world rulers of this present darkness, against the spiritual hosts of wickedness in the heavenly places" (Ephesians 6:11–12). There is indeed an evil will at loose in the world that is more than the will of any individual or of all individuals put together. This evil will has many servants at its beck and call. If we look into our own selves and see how the evil we do points to control by a will not really our own, we will know that a power stronger than ourselves and stronger than the Evil One is needed if ever we are to be free.

In the face of all these tyrants, we have the testimony of believers that a final and conclusive victory has already been won. It is like the battle of Gettysburg. Once the North had triumphed at Gettysburg, the issue was decided. Although battles continued to be waged with equal fury, there was no question about the outcome. The victory was assured. A new era had already begun. The same is true of the cross in which there already occurred "a new birth of freedom."

The cross is the sign of victory. It marks the beginning of a new age in which the tyrants of law, wrath, sin, death and the Devil have had their power broken. "I say to you, every one who commits sin is a slave to sin. The slave does not continue in the house for ever; the son continues for ever. So if the Son makes you free, you will be free indeed" (John 8:34–36).

New in Christ

The heading of this chapter is "God Makes Things New in Christ." Now our old sinful self may be buried with Christ into his death, and a new life arise with him out of that death.

Luther concludes his Explanation of the Second Article as follows: "All this he has done that I may be his own, live under him in his kingdom, and serve him in everlasting righteousness, innocence, and blessedness, just as he is risen from the dead and lives and rules eternally. This is most certainly true."

The Resurrection

Without Easter, Good Friday would be a day of darkness and utter defeat. But the resurrection of Jesus, which we celebrate on Easter, is the vindication of the victory that has been won. Jesus is "the first fruits of those who have fallen asleep" (1 Corinthians 15:20).

The Easter celebration, which occurs each spring, is quite different from the pagan celebrations of the return of spring. The annual coming of spring is, of course, cause enough for worshipful rejoicing. The new growth that occurs in spring is indeed a miracle because it is not something human powers can bring about.

The miracle of spring after the death of winter is also a symbol of the resurrection from the dead and has been rightly celebrated by all people. But Easter is not only the celebration of the return of robins and tulips. For after spring and summer comes winter in an ever recurring cycle. Though robins and tulips will return again and again, the particular robin who delighted you this year as the first sign of spring and the particular tulip that touched these particular lips will never return. They become fertilizer for the future, making place for other life.

It is, therefore, the *end* of this ever recurring cycle of birth, flowering, maturity, death, and decay that Easter celebrates. It is the death of death itself, for "the last enemy to be destroyed is death" (1 Corinthians 15:26). Easter celebrates the coming of the everlasting spring after which there shall be no more winter. In fact, Easter signals the beginning of " new heaven and a new earth."

Jesus' resurrection, then, is not merely a recurring fact of nature that we celebrate. It is a once-for-all, unique event that occurred in history, but that ran quite counter to what happens in nature. If the reality of Jesus' resurrection is denied, then the good news itself is denied as well as all that we have said about the atonement and the victory. "If Christ has not been raised, your faith is futile and you are still in your sins" (1 Corinthians 15:17).

The oldest account

The oldest account of the Resurrection in the New Testament, 1 Corinthians 15, is startling in its stark simplicity. Paul simply repeats the tradition that was handed down to him. We have to take note, however, that this tradition does not separate the event from its interpretation. Jesus' death, real as it is, is not an ordinary death. Nor is his resurrection, real as it is, just the resuscitation of a corpse. The New Testament witness is more than a report of something that happened; it is also a witness to an event which can be seen only with the eyes of faith.

Paul says, "For I delivered to you as of first importance what I also received, that Christ *died for our sins in accordance with the scriptures*" (1 Corinthians 15:3). Many persons witnessed Jesus' death on Calvary. Only those who were enlightened by the Spirit, however, believed that this death was for their sins and that it was *in accordance with the scriptures.*

Paul continues by saying that Jesus "was buried, [and] *that he was raised on the third day in accordance with the scriptures*" (1 Corinthians 15:4). In another place Paul writes that Jesus "was put to death for our trespasses *and raised for our justification*" (Romans 4:25).

The apostle enumerates those to whom, according to the tradition he knows, the risen Christ appeared. The list is quite different from the list recorded by the four evangelists. Each list represents different traditions based upon a witness that we have no way of recapturing. One thing is certain—that it very likely happened as reported. Counter to all their expectations, the disciples became convinced that Jesus was raised from the dead. This was not because they wanted to believe it and therefore hallucinated it. Nor was it because it followed logically and necessarily from who they thought he was. Nor was their belief in the Resurrection an attempt to justify their faith in Jesus by making up the whole story. No! The disciples were persuaded by what happened, which was counter to their expectations.

The Resurrection appearances should not be understood as appearances of a resuscitated corpse, which could have been seen by anyone who happened to be at the right place.

The Book of Acts tells us that Jesus appeared to chosen witnesses. "And we are witnesses to all that he did both in the country of the Jews and in Jerusalem. They put him to death by hanging him on a tree; but God raised him on the third day and made him manifest; *not to all the people but to us who were chosen by God as witnesses, who ate and drank with him after he rose from the dead. And he commanded us to preach to the people, and to testify that he is the one ordained by God to be judge of the living and dead*" (Acts 10:39–42).

The testimony of Peter in Acts makes it clear that we should not isolate the Resurrection from its meaning, from the fact that it was divinely ordained, and from the fact that it was to be preached not just as a highly unusual event of an individual returning from the dead. Such stories seem to have been a dime a dozen. Instead, the Resurrection was to be seen as an event of vital significance for all people as they confront their Maker and their Judge.

In view of that testimony, we can well afford to live with the differing New Testament records and even speak in favor of their trustworthiness.

The biblical record is remarkably free of any attempts to make the Resurrection plausible. According to the New Testament no one actually witnessed the Resurrection. For those who want to discredit the fact of the Resurrection, then, there are all kinds of explanations: Jesus was not really dead; he was revived in the cool of the tomb; his disciples stole his body. The disciples, however, were convinced by Jesus' own appearances that he was alive again after he had died. But that Jesus "was put to death for our trespasses and raised for our justification," the disciples came to know only by the enlightenment of the Holy Spirit.

In any case this record is all we have, and we will have to make the most of it. It records the turning point in the lives of a discouraged and frightened handful of disciples, who arose to become confident and joyful proclaimers of good news to all the world.

Summary statements

Below are a number of summary statements to help you recall and think about what you have read.

1. Jesus' fulfillment of the Old Testament prophecies radically corrected people's expectations about the Messiah.

2. Jesus fulfilled God's law in the sense that he embodied the life God wants his creatures to live.

3. Jesus is truly human and truly divine.

4. Jesus is the love of God spelled out in actions.

5. Jesus became flesh not just to show us what God is like, but to save us from a plight from which we could not save ourselves.

6. There are many facets to Jesus' atonement.

7. Through his life, death, and resurrection, Jesus atoned for our sins and won the victory over all the powers that are too strong for us.

8. Jesus' resurrection signals the beginning of "a new heaven and a new earth."

9. The risen Lord Jesus is present in all the world and in a special way in the church.

Word and Sacraments

"This [the church] is the assembly of all believers among whom the Gospel is preached in its purity and the holy sacraments are administered according to the Gospel."

Augsburg Confession, Article VII

Chapter Five
GOD BUILDS HIS CHURCH

What is the meaning of the Trinity? How does God build his church? What is the significance of the church? What are the means through which God directs his grace to people? Who is the Holy Spirit, and what does he do? How can a person speak of one church when there are so many different denominations? What must people do to earn God's favor? How can a person learn to pray correctly? Why is there an ordained ministry in the church?

Pentecost, which comes fifty days after Easter and which is the day the Holy Spirit was poured out on the early disciples (see Acts 2), marks the birthday of the Christian church. It is the last of the three great festivals of the Christian church year.

The church's celebration

Christmas and Easter have been adopted and modified by western culture. Only the church, however, celebrates Pentecost. Society celebrates Christmas as "the festival of the child" or of "the family." People are encouraged to show kindness to neighbors, at least at Christmastime, since this pays off in inner satisfaction. At Easter society celebrates the "return of the flowers" and the fact that "hope springs eternal in the human breast." Christmas and Easter, then, have a common, universal appeal that allows them to be celebrated by almost everyone. After all, whose heart is not softened by a "babe in a manger" and gifts of shepherds and kings? Who is not thrilled by the first flowers of spring? However, who knows what to do with that curious person of the Trinity symbolized by the dove—the Holy Spirit?

The real meaning of Christmas and Easter cannot be known except by the power of the Spirit given at Pentecost. Christmas and Easter may be celebrated by society as "universal religious symbols," but these observances must be radically corrected and fulfilled by the gospel if they are to be properly observed.

If Christmas and Easter are rightly celebrated in the church, then Pentecost will also be celebrated with equal wonder, elation, and gratitude. If not, then we have failed properly to understand the significance of the doctrine of the Trinity, the meaning of revelation, and the nature and mission of the church.

Meaning of the Trinity

Understanding the Trinity does not mean forcing ourselves to believe that one is three. The symbol of the Trinity is a triangle with three equal sides forming one figure— the Father, Son, and Holy Spirit—each fully God. The Father, who is fully God, sends the Son in whom "the whole fullness of deity dwells bodily" and who effects redemption; the Spirit procedes from the Father and the Son as the fullness of God's power and presence. Or to put it in terms of God's revelation of himself: God is the author of the revelation (Father-Revealer); God is fully present in the revelation (Son-Revelation); God himself must make you aware of himself in the revelation (Holy Spirit-Revealedness).

Jesus is present everywhere

The Book of Acts indicates that the followers of Christ, even after his resurrection appearances, did not understand the real significance of his coming into the world or of his life, death, and resurrection. When the risen Lord told the disciples to go to Jerusalem to wait for the promise of the Father to be fulfilled, they asked: "Lord, will you at this time restore the kingdom to Israel?" (Acts 1:6). They still dreamed of a return of the times of King David and of the establishment of an earthly paradise. But listen to Jesus' answer! He did not reject the idea of restoring the kingdom to Israel or of the hope for peace and justice in this life. Instead he said, "It is not for you to know times or seasons which the Father has fixed by his own authority. But you shall receive power when the Holy Spirit has come upon you; and you shall be my witnesses in Jerusalem and in all Judea and Samaria and to the end of the earth" (Acts 1:7–8). Then he left his followers and was seen no more. It was not until the Spirit descended upon the disciples at Pentecost that the meaning of all this, including their mission to the ends of the earth and to the end of the age, became clear to them. Subsequently the disciples "turned the world upside down" (Acts 17:6).

The Lord left his followers and yet did not really leave them at all. This is the significance of the Ascension. Luther said of the ascended Jesus, "Once he was far away, now he is near." As long as Jesus walked the earth as a truly human person, his presence was confined to a specific time and place. However, when he ascended into heaven to sit at the right hand of God, he did not go away to some distant place. Instead, he filled the universe from earth to sky. The right hand of God, to which we refer in the Apostles' Creed, is the hand of God's power that blesses. The God who chose not to remain in his aloofness, but who came to earth to share our life and to suffer in the man Jesus, is the One who is now everywhere present.

Nevertheless, neither you nor I nor anyone else can know that the God who is everywhere present is the God who died for us unless someone comes running with the news. This, then, raises the question of the nature and message of the church and how the risen Lord is active in the church today.

A personal confession

In Luther's Explanation of the Third Article of the Apostles' Creed his understanding of the Holy Spirit and the church becomes a personal confession. He says: "I believe that I cannot by my own understanding or effort believe in Jesus Christ my Lord, or come to him. But the Holy Spirit has called me through the Gospel, enlightened me with his gifts, and sanctified and kept me in true faith. In the same way he calls, gathers, enlightens, and sanctifies the whole Christian church on earth, and keeps it united with Jesus Christ in the one true faith. In this Christian church day after day he fully forgives my sins and the sins of all believers. On the last day he will raise me and all the dead and give me and all believers in Christ eternal life. This is most certainly true."

Of sanctification

The First Article of the Creed has been entitled "Of Creation" and the Second "Of Redemption." The Third Article has been entitled "Of Sanctification." This article has to do with how we are changed from sinners into saints by the work of the Holy Spirit, who is active in the church and whose work is completed in the resurrection of the dead.

Not our doing

The Third Article explains that we come to faith in Jesus as Lord not by our own "understanding or effort."

We believe not because we figured out the true heart of God in relation to us by sitting, thinking, and pulling ourselves out of sin's clutches. Nor because the Holy Spirit somehow beamed faith into our hearts and minds directly without any visible, earthly means.

The means of grace

Sanctification, which literally means "to make holy," is the Holy Spirit's work through the church's proclamation of the good news. Luther says, "But the Holy Spirit has called me through the Gospel, enlightened me with his gifts, and sanctified and kept me in true faith."

The Holy Spirit's work involves the church. Individuals who have been called through the gospel, gathered into congregations, and enlightened and sanctified by the Holy Spirit constitute the Christian church on earth. The Holy Spirit keeps these individuals united with Jesus the Christ in faith. In the church there is daily forgiveness, daily rebirth to newness of life, and finally resurrection to eternal life. God in his grace comes to us to build and nurture his church, not everywhere or without using earthly instruments, but where the gospel is proclaimed by living witnesses. The *Augsburg Confession*, Article VII, says: "It is also taught among us that one holy Christian church will be and remain forever. This is the assembly of all believers among whom the Gospel is preached in its purity and the holy sacraments are administered according to the Gospel."

One church

"One holy Christian church will be and remain forever" is a way of saying that there always was, is, and shall be only one church. In the Nicene Creed we confess: "We believe in one holy catholic and apostolic Church." The oneness of the church is a fact. It is a gift, not something we must still achieve.

Since, however, there are various denominations throughout the world, it follows that the *one* church must cut across the lines of all the existing Christian denominations. The one church is the hidden church. It can only be believed and confessed. This is not to imply that the church is always and completely invisible. Rather, the church consists of flesh and blood, men and women gathered together to worship God and do his will. But this one church is hidden in the sense that only God knows who are the true believers joined to each other through their common Lord. Church membership lists or baptismal certificates do not reveal who the true believers are. Nor do outward works of piety since no one can see into another's heart. As the apostle says: "If I speak in the tongues of men and of angels, but have not love, I am a noisy gong or a clanging cymbal. . . . If I give away all I have, and if I deliver my body to be burned, but have not love, I gain nothing" (1 Corinthians 13:1 and 3).

The *one* Christ also cannot be identified with any institution whether Roman Catholic, Eastern Orthodox, Lutheran, Evangelical, Presbyterian, Methodist, or Baptist. The World Council of Churches, therefore, recognizes as members those churches that confess faith in the Triune God. Moreover, since Vatican II, the Roman Church has acknowledged that the one church is not confined to its hierarchy.

We confess not only one church, but "one holy catholic and apostolic Church." The Apostles' Creed adds the words the "communion of saints." The church is holy through the forgiveness of sins. Therefore, the phrase "communion of saints" is not really something added to "one holy catholic and apostolic Church," but something that stands in apposition to it. The "communion of saints" refers to all in the church, who are saints because their sins have been covered by Jesus' righteousness.

The church is Christian because it confesses Jesus as Christ and Lord. It is also catholic or universal, because it is for all the world and for all people.

The church is apostolic because it is in continuity with the apostolic witness, not because of an unbroken line of succession from the apostles down to the present-day ordained ministry of the church.

Pure gospel

Having described the oneness of the church, the *Augsburg Confession* goes on to say that the church is "the assembly [the gathering together, the fellowship] of all believers among whom the Gospel is preached in its purity and the holy sacraments are administered according to the Gospel."

While there is difficulty in knowing just what is involved in the pure preaching of the gospel, this affirmation nevertheless says something distinctive about the nature of the church. It does not say that the church exists only where persons accept an entire system of doctrine that has been spelled out in minute detail. Doctrine, of course, is very important because actions always grow out of the basic beliefs. The framers of the *Augsburg Confession,* however, were not thinking of a system of doctrine. They were concerned about what has been called the "living voice of the gospel."

The *Augsburg Confession* says that the church comes into being and continues to be nurtured only where the good news is proclaimed. News has to do with events. Like all news, the report of events and their significance has to be rightly reported and not deliberately or inadvertently distorted. What actually happened and what is the meaning of that happening? What are its implications and consequences? Since news is reported from different perspectives and since it can be easily distorted in transmission, whether orally or in writing, the proclamation of news becomes a precarious and challenging venture. There can never be complete assurance that the task has been perfectly accomplished.

So it is with the proclamation of the good news of the crucial event that gave birth to the church and by which it continues to live. That is why we have the Scriptures, human as they are and yet divinely inspired. They are the written record of the first witnesses and the only source of and ultimate check on the pure preaching of the gospel.

Moreover, pure preaching also depends on what the listeners actually hear. This makes it doubly difficult. What assurance does any proclaimer of the good news have that in any particular situation involving particular people, he or she is really proclaiming the good news upon which salvation depends? The leaders of the Reformation were convinced by sound reasoning and by Holy Scripture, that their proclamation was right in their situation. But that does not guarantee that a mere slavish repetition of the words the Reformers used, or even the words of the Bible, will proclaim the good news rightly today. Time and place change the meaning of words. Therefore constant retranslation, not only of the Bible, but of the gospel in living proclamation, is necessary.

All these difficulties, however, only reinforce the basic fact that the church is constituted and nurtured by "the living voice of the gospel," by actual proclamation of the Word of God through the mouths of those who have heard that Word and then pass it on to others.

This makes the Word of God central to the chain of living witnesses who make up the church. Luther once said that God's people cannot be without God's Word and God's Word cannot be without God's people. In other words God's people, the church, came into being through the Word preached by chosen witnesses who had been made believers in that Word by the power of the Holy Spirit. The Word of God does not resound throughout the ages and the universe as a kind of radiowave that can be found and tuned in. Nor is that Word simply preserved as a dead letter on a printed page. It is from the lips of living witnesses that the life-giving Word is heard. So the Word of God is truly central in the church.

The *Augsburg Confession* adds, "and the holy sacraments are administered according to the Gospel." The sacraments must also be a proclamation of the gospel and not an addition to it. They cannot be something which works in a way other than the proclaimed Word.

What we have been talking about, then, is what is commonly called a ministry of Word and Sacraments. Word and Sacraments constitute the "means of grace," the means by which our gracious God makes himself available to us in the church. They are the means he uses to work faith in us and to keep us in a right relationship with himself, with ourselves, with others, and with the whole created world. They are the means through which he works all good within us, and we neglect them at our peril.

Word and Sacraments

The expression "Word and Sacraments" is deeply ingrained in the Christian tradition. Strictly speaking, there is only one means of grace by which the gracious God comes to us, that is, by his Word of address to us. This Word may, in turn, take many forms. As Luther says in the *Smalcald Articles*, Part III, Article IV: "The Gospel . . . offers counsel and help against sin in more than one way, for God is surpassingly rich in his grace: First, through the spoken word, by which forgiveness of sin (the peculiar office of the Gospel) is preached to the whole world; second, through Baptism; third, through the holy Sacrament of the Altar; fourth, through the power of keys (that is, the pronouncement of absolution); and finally, through the mutual conversation and consolation of brethren."

Public proclamation

The form of the Word we know best is public proclamation or preaching. Far too often, however, we tend to

limit this form to preaching from the pulpit. Rightly understood, preaching means every public proclamation of the
good news. It includes also the teaching that is carried on
in the church and in the name of the church. We cannot
put any limits on where the public proclamation of the
gospel may take place.

Mutual conversation and consolation

Luther distinguished between public proclamation and
what he called the "mutual conversation and consolation
of brethren" (and sisters). By this he meant all the talk that
goes on between Christians wherever and whenever it
occurs. Regardless of how essential public worship is, the
Word of God is mightily at work not only there—not only
in formal worship or teaching situations—but wherever
and whenever Christians talk about and console each
other with the good news.

Visible words

The Word of God also takes the form of sacraments,
that is, actions in which the Word of God is embodied in
visible earthly elements. Without the Word and promise of
God the earthly elements (for example, water in Baptism,
bread and wine in the Lord's Supper) are not in and of
themselves conveyors of the gospel. With the Word and
promise of God, however, they are means of grace. Since
the Word of God is a necessary and effective factor, the
sacraments with their visible elements have been called
"visible words."

It should not be forgotten that the Word is always itself
an action which accomplishes wondrous things. In the
sacraments, what the Word does is acted out. The person
whose sins are washed away by the Word in Baptism is
actually washed. The one who shares in the body and

blood of Christ in the Lord's Supper for the forgiveness of sins receives the bread and wine into his or her body.

Grace in action

Grace is always and only God's action of forgiving, renewing, and improving persons. God in his grace imparts himself through the sacraments, and in the sacraments is the fulness of the gospel. The sacraments differ from preaching and other proclamations of the gospel in that they include earthly elements that are used to act out God's gracious work and to serve as pledges of his generous gifts.

Pledges of salvation

Sacramentum is a Latin word. It was originally used to refer to the money or other valuables litigants in a court of law deposited as a guarantee of their truthfulness, which they forfeited if they were not faithful to their word. The word also referred to the oath soldiers took to their liege lords, pledging them unswerving fidelity. So it is with the visible elements in the sacraments. They serve as pledges of the truth of the Word; they are pledges that God keeps his word. As water washes the body, so does the sacramental water wash the person clean from sin. As persons receive the bread and wine into their own bodies in the Lord's Supper, so do they receive the broken body and shed blood of Christ for the remission of their sins.

This is what is meant by "sacraments . . . administered according to the Gospel." This phrase does not refer to all the minutiae—wine versus grape juice, common cup versus individual cups.

It is the Word in its different forms, including the Word in the form of sacraments, which brings the church into being and nurtures it. There is something confusing, however, about saying "Word and Sacraments" as though the sacraments were something separate from the Word and offered something other than the Word offers. Luther insisted, "The sacrament is the Gospel." While it is possible to distinguish between preaching and the sacraments and to assign each their specific role in the life of the church, they should nevertheless be understood simply as different ways in which the one God comes to us in his grace.

Justification and sanctification

Let us now be more specific about the lives of Christians within the assembly of the church.

In the first place, we must make clear that a person cannot be saved by perfectly keeping a set of rules or by achieving certain virtues. Salvation and justification are matters of relationships. Being a sinner means being in the wrong relationship with God and under his wrath and condemnation. Being justified means being in the right relationship with God because of his gracious act of forgiveness in Christ. It means being able to stand in the judgment, not because of one's own righteousness, but as Luther said, because of "the strange and foreign righteousness of Christ." Perfection, therefore, has nothing to do with our salvation. Being justified does not mean having attained perfection, but having been accepted as God's forgiven child.

Good works

Now comes the most difficult part to comprehend if we are not to end up with "cheap grace" and a "what-the-hell" attitude. If a right relationship with God is so easy, why not sin all the more so that grace might abound (Romans 6:1)? The fact is, however, we have been saved by grace so that we may do genuinely good works, not that we may sin more.

God's grace in Christ frees us from our self-centered efforts to achieve our own salvation and to try to feather our nests in heaven by doing good works. Luther's objection to the whole medieval sacramental system was that it kept people preoccupied with their own soul's salvation and their own climb to perfection. As a result they did good works, not for their neighbors, but for their own sakes. So the circle of people's self-centeredness was not broken. On the other hand, when people know they have been accepted by God in his grace in Christ, they can freely do good works without fear of punishment or hope of reward, but because of trust in God and love for their neighbor.

Newness of life

Jesus said to Nicodemus, "Unless one is born anew, he cannot see the kingdom of God" (John 3:3). There are no Christians, therefore, who have not been "born again." We have been declared forgiven in Christ, even though we are still sinners. This is inseparable from an actual rebirth. Only a good tree can bring forth good fruit, and here is the birth of the good tree. We do not become good by doing good; we must first be good before we can do good. God's gracious action in Jesus Christ makes us "good," and so we are able to do "good works." As the apostle writes, "If any one is in Christ, he is a new creation; the old has passed away, behold, the new has come" (2 Corinthians 5:17).

New and old

God's grace in Christ is by no means cheap grace for people. It does not imply perfection or the end of our struggle against unrighteousness. Although the decisive victory has been won in Christ, the war continues with equal vehemence throughout life.

We have new birth in Jesus Christ, but the old Adam or sinner is still present within us. The Christian's lifelong struggle is between the old Adam and the new. This lifelong struggle does not abate with the years. As an old man, I can vouch for that. The temptations of old age may not be the same as those in youth, but they do not lose their vigor. The possibility of falling into the abyss continues throughout life.

That is why it is important for the Christian to remain always under the Word of God, the means of grace. Then he or she will learn to be a better fighter equipped with the "whole armor of God" and "able to withstand in the evil day" (Ephesians 6:11–17).

Led by the Spirit

Some Christians believe in the direct action of the Holy Spirit apart from any external means. They wait in silence for the Spirit to move them to make a Spirit-inspired testimony. To suppose, however, that these Christians do not depend upon the proclaimed Word is an illusion because not one of them would know of Jesus the Christ except through living testimony. Whatever testimony they give that centers in Jesus the Christ is based upon the Bible, which is the record of living testimony. Christianity did not spread by the Spirit coming from within persons, but by proclaiming the news of events.

So-called "born again Christians" put great stock in their personal conversion experiences. In Luther's day these people were known as the Anabaptists. They insisted that children who had been baptized in infancy should be re-baptized after they had a conversion experience and accepted Christ as their personal Savior. In time this came to be known as "believer's baptism" and, consequently, children or infants were no longer baptized.

At an inter-seminary conference some years ago a young man said, "I have never had a religious experience and I hope never to have one." Whereupon people representing the "born again" tradition nearly went through the roof. Perhaps we can appreciate what the young man was trying to say. A person cannot put his or her faith in an inner emotional experience which is, after all, fleeting. If a prisoner has been freed from his chains, it is not a matter of how he feels. He has as a matter of fact been freed. Similarly, persons do not get assurance from an experience of assurance. That would be faith in one's own faith. Assurance comes from outside oneself. There has to be someone upon whom one can rely. The sacraments, which are actions in which God comes to us in grace, give this kind of assurance.

On the other hand, reliance upon outward, formal participation in the sacraments can easily lead to a kind of magical view of them. That too is wrong.

"Religious experience" is a useful term. We are not things to be acted upon magically, but persons who respond to a word of address. If we do not ourselves experience Jesus the Christ as our Savior, then what possible difference can he make in our lives? Experience is the medium through which God's revelation, his Word to us, must pass if it is to reach us as persons. God's action precedes our action. God loved us first. The celebration of the Lord's Supper is not merely an occasion *for us to remember* what once happened long ago, but a time of our Lord actually giving himself to us.

There can be no question that Christians must be born anew if they are to see the kingdom of God. The lives of millions of "born again Christians" testify to the radical change they have undergone. Paul may be cited as an example of born-againism because of his conversion on the Damascus road (Acts 9). Even after that experience, which changed the course of his life, it was not until years later and after much instruction and contemplation that Paul emerged as the great apostle to the Gentiles. It is not necessary that everyone have a dramatic conversion experience before they can be "born again Christians." Every genuine Christian is actually born again through God's gracious offer of forgiveness in Word and Sacrament and should be conscious of such a rebirth.

Baptism as a sacrament

Baptism may be defined as that act by which we become the forgiven children of God, heirs of salvation, and persons who are in a positive relationship with God. Our chief concern throughout life is not to lose or squander that inheritance, but to make full use of it.

Baptism is a universal religious symbol that becomes Christian when the Word is added to it. I once witnessed a ceremony in Tokyo where a couple was married at a fountain. The clear crystal waters were poured over their clasped hands. I did not understand a word that was said. The water with its cleansing and life-giving power spoke for itself. The only way I could have known whether it was a Christian Baptism would have been if I could have understood the words that were spoken.

In *The Small Catechism*, Luther says of Baptism that it "is not water only, but it is water used together with God's Word and by his command." He continues, "Water by itself is only water, but with the Word of God it is a life-giving water which by grace gives the new birth through the Holy Spirit."

We should take note of the intimate connection between the Word and the water. In fact, Luther does not hesitate to call the water itself "a life-giving water." Water serves many gracious purposes and is essential to life. Without water there is only desert. Without water we perish. Water blesses us in so many ways. For example, we plunge into it on a hot summer day. God is present in water and blesses us through it. But the water in these instances does not wash us from our sins or drown the old

Adam in us. It does this only when it is connected with God's Word and when we are baptized into the name of the Father, the Son, and the Holy Spirit, that is, into a faith-relationship with the God of the Christian revelation.

Infant Baptism

Christians baptize infants so that they may grow up in the knowledge that they are God's forgiven children in Christ. Infant Baptism is the necessary corollary to being justified by grace alone for Christ's sake through faith. It makes clear that redemption is entirely God's work, for the infant surely contributes nothing to his or her own Baptism. The infant does not choose God, but God chooses the infant child.

At the very beginning of life before the child is aware of it, there is this act of gracious deliverance backed up by the promises of God which are sure. This is why Baptism is the bulwark of the Christian life. Whenever doubts come, as Luther said, a person needs only to return to his or her Baptism and to exult, "I have been baptized!" The baptized person has the necessary confidence in the midst of insecurity because of the constant reminder of what God in his grace has done. If a person receives Baptism in infancy, he or she avoids that disastrous interval between birth and a later period when the person does not really know who he or she is. Was Christ's atoning, liberating death really for me? Am I a full member of the Christian church? Or is Baptism, a washing from sin, really not necessary for a newborn child since such a child could not possibly have committed a conscious sinful act?

We must think again of what we have said about original sin and the fact that every person is part of a sinful race. If that is understood, then the reason for infant Baptism becomes evident. If sinners can only beget sinners, then all children need to be cleansed of their sinful condition as soon as possible so that there be no interval when they do not know who they are because they do not know whose they are.

Word of God and faith

Baptism does not produce effects automatically like a chemical reaction. Baptism is a personal encounter or transaction. Therefore, Luther emphasizes the necessity of faith as much as he emphasizes that all the power and effectiveness of Baptism are in the Word of God. In answer to the question "How can water do such great things?" Luther says: "It is not the water that does these things, but God's Word with the water and our trust in this Word." Faith and trust are absolutely essential if Baptism is to be something other than an impersonal operation performed upon an object. Baptism is a personal meeting with a subject who says "I."

Think of infants who are baptized, but who cannot say "I." Can they have faith? Some have answered, "Yes, of course, they can have faith in the same way that they cling to their mothers and trust them. So do they also rest in the promises of God." This incipient "beginning-to-be" faith or seed of faith, which later grows into the full fruit of conscious faith, is like the acorn that is already the oak, provided of course, it is properly nurtured. So must the seed of faith implanted in Baptism also be nurtured.

The above is a possible answer, but it will by no means satisfy those for whom faith is a "mighty, busy, active thing," as Luther described it. It is helpful to recall the biblical view of time. In the Bible, time is not a series of empty chronological moments on a clock or calendar, but a *kairos*, a time when something happens. Baptism is the time or *kairos* of God's gracious acceptance of the sinner and the sinner's conscious response to that acceptance in faith—whenever that happens! Who knows how early in the life of a child who has been given Christian nurture this response may come. Or who knows how many years may elapse before there is that conscious response, especially if there is no Christian upbringing. Whenever it occurs, however, it is still the "time" of Baptism.

I, for example, was baptized in infancy and grew up in a Christian home. I never had a climactic conversion experience. As far back as my memory goes I grew up in the knowledge that Jesus loved me, and I felt badly and asked to be forgiven when I offended his love. As I grew up, these experiences deepened. But there also came periods of doubt, conscious revolt, and offense. Then, because I heard the Word of God again, I returned by God's grace to my Baptism and overcame my doubts. Moreover, such moments of conversion, return, and rebirth continue to be a reality for me.

Daily Baptism

Water can drown. Baptism also signifies the drowning of the old Adam and the birth of the new person. This drowning and new birth is by no means once-and-for-all. It must occur daily. That is the lifelong significance of Baptism. The Christian's life is not a growth toward perfection; it is not supposing that once you have found Christ your troubles are over for good. The Christian's life is a continuing struggle, not having attained, but always pressing toward the prize of our high calling in Jesus Christ. This continuing struggle underscores the necessity for us to remain at all times under the influence of the means of grace and the assurance of God's presence and blessing.

The Lord's Supper

The Lord's Supper may be defined as *that act by which God would strengthen his baptized children in their relation to him and to each other.* Gustaf Aulen in *The Faith of the*

Christian Church calls the Lord's Supper "the sacrament of suffering and victorious love." In it we receive the benefits of Christ's death and celebrate victory, for it is the risen Christ who is present with us at his Table.

Over the years, scholars have debated whether the Lord's Supper was actually instituted as a Passover meal. To date there has been no final agreement on the matter. Nevertheless, it is quite generally recognized that the Lord's Supper must be interpreted as both a correction and a fulfillment of the ancient Passover meal. Jesus' early followers were Jews for whom the celebration of the Passover commemorated both their release from Egyptian bondage and their constitution as a free people. However, since in Jesus' time they were again in bondage, this time to the Romans, the Passover was an occasion to look forward to a deliverance still to come.

Their Passover celebration, therefore, had a threefold reference: (1) it reminded them of the bitterness of Egyptian bondage and God's great and gracious act of deliverance; (2) it assured them that this same Lord God who delivered them was present with them in that meal in which they partook of the Passover Lamb, whose blood had been the occasion of their deliverance; and (3) since they were still under the yoke of an alien lord, they looked forward to the time when the Messiah would come with an even greater deliverance. Every celebration of that meal included the question by the youngest member of the household, Why do we celebrate this feast?

The celebration of the Lord's Supper has a similar threefold reference. Paul writes, "For as often as you eat this bread and drink the cup, you proclaim the Lord's death until he comes" (1 Corinthians 11:26). "As often as you eat this bread and drink the cup" refers to the presence of the Deliverer God in Jesus the Christ. "You proclaim the Lord's death" is a backward look to Calvary. "Until he comes" is a forward look toward face-to-face fellowship with God in the new heaven and the new earth, which will be ushered in at Christ's return.

A memorial

Some have regarded the Lord's Supper merely as a memorial of a past event. The Lord's Supper is truly an act of remembrance. Jesus said, "Do this in remembrance of me" (Luke 22:19). That is to say, the whole action of giving thanks and sharing the bread and cup was to be done not in remembrance of deliverance from Egypt, but in remembrance of Jesus himself. It was to be done in remembrance of that great act of deliverance and victory on Calvary, which was sealed by Jesus' resurrection from the dead. The Lord's Supper, therefore, is in memory of the actual historical event that inaugurated "the new age" in Jesus Christ.

This act of remembrance, however, is not just recalling a past event that grows dimmer as time goes on. The saving and victorious event of Christ's death for our sins and his rising again for our justification *becomes contemporary only in faith*. Those who were with Jesus in the upper room on the night of his betrayal had not yet experienced Calvary or Easter morn. When they stood on Calvary's hill and watched Jesus die, they did not realize that his death was for the sins of the world. Nor did they, when the risen Christ appeared to them, experience this as his victory over death for all the world. They recognized this later in the power of the Holy Spirit. In other words, the saving event and the victory of Jesus Christ became contemporary for them only through faith. So also through faith are we there when they crucified our Lord so that the body that was broken for the world is broken for us now, and the blood that was then shed is now poured out for us.

Real presence

Lutherans have always insisted on the "real presence" of Christ in the Holy Communion. This insistence was originally intended to counteract the idea that Christ was present in only a "spiritual" sense. Some said only the "spirit" of the crucified and risen Christ was present in the sacrament, not his real flesh and blood.

Others advocated the idea that Christ was present in the sacrament only in his divine nature as true God and not in his human nature as true man. But it was Jesus Christ, true God and true man, who suffered and died on Calvary and who rose again from the dead and ascended to the right hand of God in order to be present everywhere. It is, then, this everywhere-present, truly divine and human Jesus Christ who comes to us at the communion table and gives himself to us in the bread and wine for the remission of sins. Of course he is also present at every meal to which we invite him when we pray "Come, Lord Jesus be our guest." He blesses us through the food we eat and the companionship we share. But unless this meal is in remembrance of the night in which he was betrayed, and the bread and the wine are distributed with the words "given and shed for you for the remission of sins," the meal is not a sacrament. Only when the Word and promise of God accompany the giving of the bread and the wine do we receive Christ's body and blood broken and shed for us. Otherwise, as Luther once suggested, we could go into the nearest tavern and swill down quantities of the blood of Christ.

The broken body and the shed blood of the sacrament are not just that of a person, even a perfect person. They are, rather, the body and blood of the God-Man—not for an earthly freedom, but for eternal freedom—not for a limited number of persons, but for all people—not in a sacrifice that has to be repeated again and again, but in a once-for-all-sufficient sacrifice. This broken body and shed blood are, therefore, available for all time and for all people. "The true body and blood of Christ," says the *Augsburg Confession,* "are really present in the Supper of our Lord under the form of bread and wine and are there distributed and received."

Future reference

Now we must talk about the future. Think of the Lord's Supper as a table fellowship and all that this implies: a time for the sharing of food and memories; a time for sorrow as well as joy; a time of peace and of being with those to whom you are bound with unbreakable bonds. But the Lord's Supper is also a time for looking into the future. We look forward to the time when we will share this fellowship again. We are aware of the many failures of that fellowship, and so we look forward to a more perfect one. We partake of the Lord's Supper now with only a fragment of the great family of God and with a Lord whom we recognize only in faith, but we look forward in hope to joining in the great marriage feast of the Lamb.

Prayer

As we look to the future, we address our concerns about it and other matters to God in prayer. There is no question that prayer is essential in the lives of Christian people. In prayer we express our dependence upon God by asking him for all that we need. We also express our thanks and praise to him.

A major portion of the church's prayers are intercessory, that is, prayers on behalf of others. The church intercedes for all who are in need, for those in authority, for those who do the world's works at great risk, and for those who are victims of disasters and of humanity's injustice.

The life of the church is inconceivable without prayer. There is no question that God does indeed bless us in many ways in answer to our prayers. In addition, we recognize that he himself must teach us how to pray. "Likewise the Spirit helps us in our weakness; for we do not know how to pray as we ought, but the Spirit himself intercedes for us with sighs too deep for words" (Romans 8:26). Our prayers may be motivated by selfishness; they may be for entirely the wrong things. They may be spoken in rebellion and offense when we cry out against God. It is only by the help of the Spirit, then, that our prayers can possibly be what they ought to be. When the Holy Spirit teaches us to pray, he does so through the Word of God that alone corrects, enlightens, and empowers us.

Whatever comes to us from God in his grace by way of answer to our prayers is really mediated to us by the Word. For God speaks to us through the Word and in it addresses our deepest needs.

Ordained ministry

The proclamation of the Word is central in the church. However, if anyone who knows the gospel can proclaim it with equal effectiveness ("the priesthood of all believers"), we may ask, Why, then, do we have an ordained ministry?

Ministers are persons who have been called and ordained to the holy office of the public proclamation of the Word and the administration of the sacraments. This office has been instituted in order that the Word might be rightly proclaimed and that the church might be nurtured by that Word decently and in order. When the congregation meets for worship, not everyone is to shout at the same time like merchants shouting their wares in a marketplace. Furthermore, when the congregation meets for the Lord's Supper, someone must preside over the celebration.

Ordination to the office of the ministry does not confer a different or higher status upon the ordained person as distinct from the rest of the laity. (Laity means literally "the people of God.") There is no higher status than being a baptized child of God. The ministry is a functional office involving the public proclamation of the Word and administration of the sacraments. This does not relieve unordained persons of the exercise of their priesthood wherever they happen to be—parents in the home, workers on the job, and the like.

The ordained ministry, however, does require special abilities and special training for specific tasks, which vary according to circumstances. Because of the office ordained ministers hold and the training they have received, they also bear a unique responsibility for the right proclamation of the gospel. But they share that responsibility with every Christian.

Although persons must feel the desire to serve the church as ordained ministers, the call to the office is mediated from God through the church. God, through the church, calls ministers. Without such a call from the church, no person can presume to minister publicly in and for the church. Nor can the church be the church without the institution of the ministry. The minister, however, has no authority in his or her person. All the power and authority of the ministry are in the Word that is proclaimed and shared.

Work in the world

The church is brought into being and nurtured by the Word of God. Christians will therefore not neglect regular worship with the people of God where the Word is proclaimed and the sacraments administered according to Christ's command. They will assemble to give expression to their praise and thanks and to bring their petitions to the throne of grace.

Constant nurture by the Word of God is not just individual nurture in order to save that person for heaven. We are justified by grace alone for Christ's sake through faith *unto good works*. These works are to be manifested in the world by each person in those places where that person happens to be. In the church we are again and again freed and empowered for our work in the world even though we are no longer of the world. As recipients of God's grace in Christ we are in and for the world, even though we are no longer "conformed to this world" (Romans 12:2).

Summary statements

Below are a number of summary statements drawn from this chapter. These statements intend to help you recall and think about what you have just read.

1. The real meaning of Christmas and Easter cannot be known except in the power of the Spirit given at Pentecost.

2. Jesus is present everywhere.

3. The Holy Spirit calls people to faith in Jesus the Christ through the gospel.

4. We cannot come to faith in Jesus as Lord by our own understanding or effort.

5. The oneness of the church is a fact, not something we must still achieve.

6. The church is one, holy, catholic, and apostolic.

7. The church comes into being and continues to be nurtured only where the good news is proclaimed.

8. The church exists wherever the gospel is preached in its purity and the sacraments are administered according to the gospel.

9. Word and Sacraments constitute the means by which our gracious God makes himself available to us in the church.

10. The sacraments are actions in which the Word of God is embodied in visible earthly elements and through which we receive the forgiveness of sins and strengthening of our faith.

11. Preaching and the sacraments are different ways in which the one God comes to us in grace.

12. Striving for perfection has nothing to do with our salvation.

13. We have been saved by grace that we may do genuinely good works.

14. Baptism is the initiating sacrament; the Lord's Supper is the nurturing sacrament that presupposes Baptism.

15. The Holy Spirit helps our prayers be what they ought to be.

16. Ordination to the office of ministry does not confer a different or higher status upon the ordained person as distinct from the rest of the laity.

17. Constant nurture by the Word of God in the church frees and empowers us for our work in the world.

Resurrection and Eternal Life

"I am the resurrection and the life."

John 11:25

Chapter Six
GOD BRINGS HIS KINGDOM

When and how will the world come to an end? What happens to people when they die? Will there be a resurrection from the dead? When will God's kingdom or rule begin? How will a person spend eternity? What is the goal of all history? Should people give up on the present as they look toward the end of the world?

A popular slogan of more optimistic times was "Building the Kingdom of God on Earth." The mission of the church was thought of as making this earth a better place in which to live. Marxist communism held forth the inevitability of a time when there would be justice on the earth and each person would contribute according to his or her ability and receive according to his or her needs. Other claims concerning evolutionary progress grew out of spectacular advances of science. People believed that every day in every way humankind was getting better and better.

Such optimism, however, was shattered by the catastrophic events of this century. Today we hear dire predictions of economic collapse, nuclear destruction, pollution of the environment, and the end of life on this planet. Nevertheless, some still find reason for optimism provided humanity uses its ingenuity and rearranges its priorities.

Last things

Books on Christian teaching have generally ended with a section on *eschatology* (pronounced es ka TAHL oh jee), which literally means "the word concerning the end." In this section theologians dealt primarily with what happens to individuals after death and what happens to the course of history itself. How will it all end? Sometimes this chapter was an addition, not integrally connected with what had gone before. There was also a tendency to neglect the end times altogether, leaving these matters to the sects who talked about "the millennium" and "the return of Christ" in a literalistic way that did not do justice to the biblical witness.

This book, however, has been written from the conviction that the end must appear already at the beginning as far as the individual's destiny and the outcome of history are concerned. We have said that humankind was made for everlasting fellowship with God and that God is not only the Creator of the world, but also the Guarantor of its fulfillment. We have described the work of Christ as an act of victory marking the beginning of a new age. The Lord's Supper was depicted as a foretaste of full, face-to-face fellowship with God. Far from redemption being regarded as escape from this world to another real world, we have said that this world in which God became incarnate in Christ is the real world. When Christ comes again in glory, he will come to this earth and establish "a new heaven and a new earth."

We may add to this the picture of the new Jerusalem coming from heaven to earth as a bride adorned for her husband, a city wherein righteousness dwells (Revelation 21:1–4). There people will have no need of the sun, for the Lord God will be their sun (Revelation 21:23). There prophecies regarding a time of justice and peace will be fulfilled—nations "shall beat their swords into plowshares, and their spears into pruning hooks" (Isaiah 2:4); nature shall no longer be red with tooth and claw, for "the wolf shall dwell with the lamb, and the leopard shall lie down with the kid, and the calf and the lion and the fatling together, and a little child shall lead them" (Isaiah 11:6). The whole creation that groans in travail for the glorious liberty of the children of God shall be delivered (Romans 8:21–22).

It remains, then, to sum up that which was there from the beginning. Indeed, we have to see everything that has gone before in the light of this promised future.

Individual destiny

Concerning the individual, we have rejected the notion of an immortal soul and have spoken instead of the resurrection of the body. Our hope for life hereafter rests upon Christ's victory over death and God's power to bring life out of death, not upon an indestructible soul within us. It is the entire person, therefore, who shall live again at God's call. This resurrection of the body does not mean a reassembling of the chemical particles that have constituted our bodies here. When Paul was aked, "How are the dead raised? With what kind of body do they come?" (1 Corinthians 15:35), he spoke of a radical transformation from what is perishable to what is imperishable, from dishonor to glory, from weakness to power, from a physical body to a spiritual body (1 Corinthians 15:42–44). He said that God would give to each creature an appropriate body. We will therefore really have to trust him, who first brought light and life into being, to bring about also this radical transformation.

The idea of the resurrection of the body has troubled many people because they have seen how the body decays. It is therefore easier for them to believe that the soul leaves the body at death and survives. The body is in the grave, but the soul has gone to heaven. The resurrection of the body, then, will not occur until the end of the world.

119

The Bible speaks of the dead as "those who are asleep" (1 Thessalonians 4:13). On the other hand, Paul speaks of being at home with the Lord once we leave this earthly dwelling (2 Corinthians 5:1–5). Martin Luther said that when the last trumpet sounds, God will stand over his grave and say "Martin, get up!" Still, when his little son was on his death bed, Luther spoke to him about how wonderful it would be in heaven with all kinds of toys to play with. He did not talk about a long wait; he indicated that heaven and toys were immediately in store for his son.

Adding to this ambiguity are Jesus' remarks about his Father's house in which there are many mansions. He said, "When I go and prepare a place for you, *I will come again* and will take you to myself, that where I am you may be also" (John 14:3). The Lord's Supper, as we have already pointed out, was celebrated in anticipation of a fellowship that would come at the end of time, after the judgment day. Yet to the thief on the cross Jesus said, "Today you will be with me in Paradise" (Luke 23:43).

I think we can clarify this matter without giving up the conviction that the entire person (body, soul, and spirit) is raised and transformed. To do this we need once again to take into account the biblical view of time. A little boy in a comic strip says: "Mommy, what time is it?" She answers: "It's half past two." The boy replies: "I don't mean that kind of time. I mean is it 'nap time' or 'lunch time' or 'play time' or 'the time when daddy comes home?' " In a similar manner we could distinguish between "wristwatch time," by which we measure the hours as they pass by, and "alarm clock time," which arouses us for work, study, and other activities.

In the Bible time is always a moment when something happens: seedtime or harvest, a time when there is still opportunity or a time when it is too late, a time for work or a time for play, a time when you are on trial or a time when the judgment has come. The time in which we now live is finite time, a time when we must live by faith and not by sight, a time when we are on trial, a time during which there is still opportunity. But then comes death, which means for us the end of this kind of time. Death is the time of judgment. For those who already in this life entered into the new age, death is, so to speak, "the time when daddy comes home." The time of waiting is over; the time of fulfillment has come in which our present concepts of space and time are inadequate. "Now we see in a mirror dimly, but then face to face. Now I know in part; then I shall understand fully, even as I have been fully un-understood" (1 Corinthians 13:12).

Already-not-yet

There has been a difference of opinion about when the kingdom or rule of God begins. Does it begin for us on this earth when we come to faith in Christ? Or does God's kingdom come only after death or when Christ returns?

We have already answered this question for the individual in our discussions about the new age ushered in by Christ's victory and our entry into that age through Baptism. As we are born again in faith and enter into a new relationship with God through Christ, we are already in God's kingdom. In faith we have already stood in the judgment. Now it remains for us to meet our Maker face-to-face and pass through the final judgment.

We may therefore characterize our condition with the phrase "already now, but not yet." The "already now" gives us "the peace of God which passes all understanding." The "not yet," however, keeps us always on the alert and does not allow us to rest on our oars.

Life and fulfillment

Some people wonder how they will spend time in heaven. Sitting forever in a rocking chair strumming our harps with properly calloused fingers carries little or no appeal for us. The fact is that the endlessness of eternal life confronts us with an idea too big for our little minds to comprehend. Eternity can only fill our hearts with awe.

How we spend that eternity in heaven, then, is something we will have to leave to God. He made the marvel of the human hand, mind, and heart together with all the other mysteries of the universe. Eternity is another element in our great faith venture. "No eye has seen, nor ear heard, nor the heart of man conceived, what God has prepared for those who love him" (1 Corinthians 2:9).

History's end and goal

It has been said that the goal of history lies beyond history. In other words, history moves both toward an end (Latin *finis*, which means "the end point") and a goal (Greek *telos*, which means "the fulfillment of a purpose").

The goal of history is the perfected kingdom of God where God is recognized as king and his will is done. To use another symbol, the goal of history is the completed table fellowship of the heavenly king. This is a symbol of inexhaustible depth and power when we think of all that even an earthly table fellowship can mean. We could describe this fellowship in terms of right relationships with God, one's self, our neighbor, and the created world. Luke writes, "And men will come from east and west, and from north and south, and sit at table in the kingdom of God" (Luke 13:29).

All of this is in line with what we said earlier about time. When a person dies, the time of struggle is over and the time of fulfillment has come. So it is with the whole course of history, which likewise consists of a time of struggle and of working toward a goal. Finally, however, history will be over, and time itself will come to an end, we know not when or how. But the "new heaven and earth" will continue. This is the meaning of Christ's coming again.

His coming brings history to its end, but also to its fulfillment or goal in "the new heaven and the new earth."

Fulfilled future and the present

During my lifetime I have seen the pendulum of optimism regarding the future versus pessimism regarding the future swing back and forth a number of times. Before the outbreak of World War I, the mood among the church's theologians was predominantly optimistic, carried by a general belief in progress. Then came a return to what is called "biblical realism" and the recognition that as the possibilities for good increase, so do the possibilities for evil. The human condition does not change, and individual persons as well as humankind in its entirety always stand at the point where the possibility of wrong decisions exist. At the same time there is the recognition that as persons make their decisions, either cohesive or divisive structures may develop. At one point in history the structures of grace may predominate, resulting in a relatively stable society. At other times demonic structures may take over as, for example, in the days of the Hitler tyranny.

All of this calls into question the possibility of ever attaining a world of perfect peace and justice. By no means does this imply that efforts toward peace, the elimination of poverty and hunger, and equal opportunity for all to develop to their full potential should be abandoned. The elimination of racism, sexism, ageism, and the like, toward which all people of good will strive today, should be pursued with all possible vigor. The possibility of a greater measure of peace and justice in the world cannot be denied. In fact, the more realistic you are about the forces working against you, the greater the measure of your achievement. It is precisely when you become unrealistic about the power of evil in the world that those forces take over.

For example, if humanity is to survive, it is imperative that some way other than war be found to settle international differences. War between nations equipped with weapons that could annihilate their opponents many times over spells total destruction. However, it is unrealistic to suppose that if one nation had the courage to disarm totally and not strike back, all nations would follow suit and lay down their arms. This is a misapplication of Jesus' injunction in the Sermon on the Mount when he says, "If any one strikes you on the right cheek, turn to him the other also" (Matthew 5:39). In the Sermon on the Mount, Jesus does not lay down rules of conduct to be followed like a rulebook for a football game. Instead, he gives examples of how love acts under certain circumstances. He provides models of love. For example, love does not strike back in anger when struck; it does not strike back even if it means being struck again.

There are many situations where love demands this kind of nonviolence. But there are other situations as well. Love may demand that order be kept. That is why Paul says (Romans 13:1–7) that the government is authorized by God to restrain the evildoer and to reward those who do good. But then he goes right on to say, "Owe no one anything, except to love one another" (Romans 13:8).

In a world in which there are persons who abuse their God-given freedoms, there must continue to be those who are authorized to keep order and to enforce justice. Even after Blacks won the right to sit in the front of a bus by non-violent means, they depended upon the law to enforce that right in the future.

All of this is to show that biblical realism reckons with the presence of evil and the necessity to struggle against it in many ways if a greater measure of justice and peace is to be attained. Recently, however, some have described this kind of realism as defeatism and throwing in the sponge. Consequently a "theology of hope" was forged which said that because the future of God is a fulfilled creation and "a new heaven and a new earth," even though this will not occur until history itself is over, there is nevertheless hope for this present world. Accordingly, a world of peace and justice, equality of opportunity, and the absence of hunger and poverty is a realistic possibility if only we pray, work, and trust in God.

There is every reason to take hope for the world seriously and to encourage and support the possibilities of what can be achieved. We dare not give in to cynicism which says, "It's no use. That's the way the world is and we'll never change it. Therefore, we will put our hope in heaven and give up on this world." Such an orientation is indeed unbiblical and unchristian if we really trust Jesus and the power of his resurrection.

It seems to me that biblical realism demands both the recognition of demonic possibilities of evil and the possibilities for good. We may set no limits to what may be achieved where the promises of God are taken seriously. However, individuals must reckon throughout their lives with the presence of the old Adam in them if they are not suddenly to suffer a grievous fall. "Let any one who thinks that he stands take heed lest he fall" (1 Corinthians 10:12). At the same time, Christians strive constantly toward the goal of their high calling in Christ. Regarding life in this world, Christians must always know that the forces of evil are mightily at work even as they trust in the power of God to achieve great things.

This is the realism of Christians who believe that the final victory has been won, that the coming of the kingdom is assured, but that the war against demonic powers must still go on.

The biblical symbol of "the millennium" (a period of peace associated with Christ's return in glory) reminds us that we should not give up on this world. The symbol of Armageddon, the great and final battle that will rage most furiously just before the final day, reminds us of the possibility that we face a conflict between the forces of evil and good, a conflict greater than any the world has ever known. This is biblical realism.

We believe that Jesus has come to inaugurate the new age. We believe that we now live in two ages at once. We believe that ultimately the old age will pass away and the promises of God will all be fulfilled.

Therefore the New Testament ends with the promise of our Lord, "Surely I am coming soon." And we pray fervently, "Amen. Come, Lord Jesus!" (Revelation 22:20).

Summary statements

Below are a number of statements drawn from this chapter to help you recall and think about what you have read.

1. We need to understand ourselves and all of history in the light of God's promises about history's end and goal.

2. There is reason for optimism even though we hear so many dire predictions regarding the fate of our world.

3. According to Romans 8, the whole creation groans in travail for the glorious liberty of the children of God— and will be delivered!

4. Hope for a life hereafter rests upon Christ's victory over death and God's power to bring life out of death.

5. The time in which we now live is finite time; in eternity, time as we now know it will be irrelevant.

6. We cannot possibly know all the good things God has in store for those who love him.

7. We are already in God's kingdom through our Baptisms; now it remains for us to meet our Maker face to face and pass through the final judgment.

8. The goal of history is the perfected kingdom of God where God is recognized as king and his will is done.

9. The whole course of history consists of a time of struggle and of working toward a goal.

10. We live in two ages at once and, consequently, work for justice and peace in this world even as we look toward the fulfillment of all things in Christ, who will come again in glory to judge the living and the dead.